I0427778

CONTENTS

CHAPTER 1

THE CAUCASUS EMIRATE JIHADISTS: THE SECURITY AND STRATEGIC IMPLICATIONS

Gordon M. Hahn

In 1994, before the outbreak of the first post-Soviet Russo-Chechen war, Shamil Basaev, the leading operative of the then self-declared independent Chechen Republic of Ichkeriya (ChRI), took a group of some 30 men from his battalion of Abkhaz fighters to Osama bin Laden's al-Qaeda (AQ) training camps in Khost, Afghanistan.[1] From this fleeting but nevertheless seminal contact between the ChRI and AQ, an increasingly closer relationship gradually developed between Chechen as well as other Caucasus nationalist and Sufi Islamic insurgents on the one hand, and AQ and the burgeoning global jihadi revolutionary movement on the other. After more than a decade of evolution, this trend culminated in the full "Salafization" or "takfirization" of the ChRI's ideology and the jihadization of its goals, operations, and tactics.[2] With the dissolution of ChRI by its then President Dokku "Abu Usman" Umarov in October 2007 and his creation of the Caucasus Emirate (CE) in its place, the Salafization and jihadization processes were made official.

We can point to a series of factors that for more than a decade drove the radicalization and jihadization of the Chechen/Caucasus mujahedin. These factors include: the influence of the global jihadi revolutionary movement and ideology realized through the Internet and other means; brutal Russian warfighting and counterinsurgency methods; the North Caucasus's colonial experience at the hands of the Russians; the region's relatively low standard of living and socioeconomic development; corrupt and ineffective local and Russian governance; and, Caucasus customs of blood revenge and martial courage. What is clear is that the CE is an explicitly self-identified global jihadist organization. Somewhat belatedly in May 2011, the CE was placed on the U.S. State Department's list of specially designated international terrorist organizations.

Still, the overwhelming weight of journalistic, analytical, and academic work on the violence in the North Caucasus tends to avoid mention of the global jihad's role in the region, the attractiveness of jihadism to a consistent portion of youth across the entire umma, or the influence of these factors on the CE's ideology, goals, strategy, and tactics. The focus is almost always on factors related to Russian responsibility for the generically named violence: the form of siloviki brutality, poor governance, and economic dependence and limited investment in the region's development. Given this chapter's purpose of providing a strategic threat assessment of the current CE insurgency in Russia's North Caucasus and its broader regional implications, it will focus on the CE's theo-ideology, goals, strategies, tactics, and capacity to deliver violence inside Russia. Given the CE's new place within the global jihadi revolutionary alliance, I will also look at the CE's broader strategic regional and global security implications.

THE CAUCASUS EMIRATE: THEO-IDEOLOGY, GOALS, STRATEGY, AND OPERATIONAL CAPACITY

The CE's ideology and goals are now defined entirely by the global jihadi revolutionary movement's Salafi takfirism and jihadism. They have broadened exponentially to include not only the internationalist aspirations of the global jihadi revolutionary alliance but also an expanded vision of the CE's territorial claims. Those claims now extend beyond the pan-Caucasus goal of the emirate to all of Russia's Muslim lands, defined so broadly as to encompass all of Russia for all intents and purposes. Operationally, I discuss the CE's wide range of tactics, including the use of the typically jihadi istishkhad, that is, martyrdom or suicide operations.

The CE's Salafist Theo-Ideology.

The Salafist theo-ideology made serious inroads beginning in the inter-war period and reached critical mass in 2002 when a ChRI shura subordinated the ChRI constitution to Shariah law, approved a strategy of bringing jihad to the entire North Caucasus, and appointed the Islamist-oriented Abdul Khalim Sadulaev as Chairman of both the new ruling Madzhli-sul Shura's Shariah Law Committee and the Shariah Court, and designated him successor to ChRI president and former Soviet general Aslan Maskhadov.[3] With Umarov's declaration of the CE in October 2007, the monopoly of the Salafist theo-ideology and its violent universal jihadism over the North Caucasus mujahedin was fully secured and institutionalized. The

CE's ideology is now precisely the same Salafist theo-ideology as that proselytized by AQ and other groups in the global jihadi revolutionary alliance (global jihad) and movement.

The key elements of this theo-ideology are tawhid, takfir, jihad, and martyrdom. These principles have been elaborated upon in great detail by three successive CE Shariah Court qadis (judges or magistrates). Of the three, it was the CE's first Shariat Court qadi "Seifullah" Anzor Astemirov, who most effectively propagated the principles of *tawhid* and *takfir*. Astemirov, like many of the CE's young generation of leaders, studied Islam abroad in the late 1990s before turning to Salafism and jihadism. Appointed by CE amir Umarov as the CE's qadi in early 2008, Astemirov founded the website, *Islamdin.com*, which incorporated his library of foreign Salafi jihadi texts, audiotapes, and videos.[4] By then, *Islamdin.com* and the other CE vilaiyats' websites carried jihadi literature exclusively, including numerous translations of the writings of leading radical Saudi, Egyptian, Iraqi, and Pakistani jihadist theologians, ideologists, and propagandists, including AQ's Osama bin Laden and Ayman al-Zawahiri;[5] the American Yemeni-based AQ in the Arabian Peninsula (AQAP) leader Anwar Al-Awlaki; and, tens of others.[6] CE sites now post Russian-language summaries and translations of editions of and articles from AQ's English-language journal *Inspire* and within days of bin Laden's death published at least 15 articles, announcements, and testimonials.[7]

Among the most prominent of the foreign jihadi theo-ideologists who Astemirov featured on *Islamdin.com* was the Jordanian Sheikh Abu Muhammad Asem al-Maqdisi. According to the United States Military Academy's Combating Terrorism Center

(CTC) among others, Maqdisi is "the most influential living Jihadi Theorist" and "the key contemporary ideologue in the Jihadi intellectual universe," and his website *Minbar al-Jihad wa'l-Tawhid* is "al-Qa`ida's main online library" and "very representative of Jihadi literature."[8] Astemirov and Maqdisi struck up a close student-mentor relationship of correspondence and consultations that would cement the CE's alliance with AQ and the global jihadi revolutionary movement. Astemirov translated and generously cited Maqdisi's works. Astemirov's key video lecture "On Tawhid" was based on Maqdisi's *Millat Ibrahim* (*The Religion of Abraham*), both becoming staples on CE and other jihadi websites.[9] Maqdisi's website began publishing articles about the CE, which were translated into Russian and posted on CE sites.[10] Maqdisi endorsed the CE in September 2009 as a fervent global jihadi organization, praising Astemirov for his Islamic knowledge.[11] In September 2010 Maqdisi urged Muslims to support the CE, "so the Emirate becomes the door to Eastern Europe."[12] Since then, the CE has entered Europe.

The theological elements of tawhid and takfir are encoded in Shariah law on the basis of the Koran and Sunna as interpreted by true (and self-selected) Salafi leaders. They have profound political, economic, and operational implications, since they define jihadists' political ideology and goals and thereby their militarily strategy and tactics.[13] *Tawid*, or strict monotheism, requires that Muslims worship only Allah; even worship of, or prayers to the Prophet Mohammed are forbidden. This puts the CE's ideology within the mainstream of global jihadism but decidedly at odds with the North Caucasus's chief Islamic tendency, Sufism, which holds a prominent place for prayer to Sufi saints and teachers, the creation of shrines at their graves, and prayers to the Prophet Mohammed. Tawhidism's call to "raise the word" or "raise the religion of Allah above all others" influences every aspect of the jihadi theo-ideology and political philosophy. It renders all other ideologies and identities — democracy, communism, socialism, nationalism, and class or ethnic identity — to be sacrilegious. Its exclusivist focus on the Deity's will for guidance in all matters, presupposes the possibility that this will is made privy to the movement's leaders, opening the way to a totalitarian monopoly over thought and power.

Much as international communism's party of professional revolutionaries were afforded a vanguard role in divining what was best for the proletariat, under jihadist theo-ideology the power to interpret Allah's will devolves by default to a small coterie of leaders (amirs), theologians (ulema and qadis), and ideologists among the mujahedin, regarded as the most devout and committed of the umma's Muslims. The special knowledge, faith, and commitment of the mujahedin vanguard — the amirs and qadis — justify their monopoly on the interpretation of the Koran and Sunna. According to Astemirov and other jihadists, the amirs, advised by Shariah court qadis, possess dictatorial powers to take unilateral decisions on the most important questions, such as that taken by Umarov in formation of the CE. The CE amir holds the ultimate reins in a circular flow of power, as he appoints the amirs and qadis for each of its largest substructures — the CE vilaiyats (from the Arabic word "welaiyat" for provinces or governates). The amir cannot be challenged on any decision unless he is deemed by a qadi to have deviated from Shariah law as interpreted by the qadi whom he has appointed.[14] The qadis' authority to advise and confirm the decisions of the amirs gives them great power. CE and some vilaiyat qadis have passed death sentences, some of which have been carried out.[15] Not surprisingly then, Astemirov and other jihadi leaders regard democratic institutions and primary allegiance to country or nationality as major deviations from monotheism and thus sacrilege, even manifestations of nonbelief. Similarly, all other philosophies, allegiances or interests that intervene between the all-knowing amirs and qadis and their interpretation of the holy texts are forbidden, since they undermine Muslims' unity in their fight against nonbelief and, more to the point, undermine their monopoly over interpretation of the Koran and Sunna, the foundations of Shariah law. Thus, nationalism is rejected as a legitimate ideological basis and is regarded as a manifestation of nonbelief, for it places the religion of Islam below ethnicity.[16]

Among Salafists and jihadists violating the principle of tawhid by worshipping these false gods leads to what is the second basic building block of the global jihad's and the CE's theology, takfirism, a trend informed by an extremely exclusivist definition of what constitutes true Islam and a real Muslim. The designation of takfir means the excommunication from the Islamic religious community and is reserved for those Muslims who are deemed to have violated fundamental tenets of Islam, such as tawhid, in accordance with Salafist interpretation. Many takfirists hold that those ruled apostates may be subject to the death penalty. Given the extremist nature of their monotheism, tawhidists and jihadists have a low threshold in deciding who should be designated takfir and subjected to the harshest of penalties. For Astemirov and the CE, those who help the Russian infidel and those who practice Sufism are at risk of takfir denunciation.[17]

7

The iconoclastic nature of the battle between those who observe the supposedly true Salafi version of Islam and those who do not, whether Muslim or infidel, leads to the jihadist's third main principle: a kinetic rather than contemplative definition of jihad and an offensive rather than defensive global jihadism. Rather than Islam's traditional emphasis on the greater jihad of the inner search for faith in Allah, takfirists require that all Muslims support to the best of their ability an Islamic war against nonbelievers, whether Christian, Jew, Hindu, secularist or any other non-Muslim religion, as well as fallen Muslim apostates; otherwise, they themselves can be subject to takfir and be deemed targets of the jihad. The implication of takfirism is that the world is divided into two camps: the takfiri jihadists and everyone else. The catholic nature of this schism combines with the general trend toward globalization fostered by technology to push Salafists towards a global rather than a local vision of jihad. Since neither ethnicity nor state borders can trump the principle of raising Islam's word above all others, the jihad cannot be confined to specific regions or targeted attacks; it must be carried out globally. Given the maximalist, sacred, and twilight nature of the struggle between the abode of Islam and the abode of the infidel in the takfirist jihadis' vision, the jihadists permit themselves rather extremist methods to maximize their capacity to attain the goal. Using Islamic holy texts' frequent praise for martyrdom in battle with the infidel during the early centuries of Islam's expansion across the Arabian Peninsula and beyond, jihadists routinely proselytize, train, and deploy the ultimate form of self-sacrificial martyrdom, (istishkhad)—that is, suicide operations. The ability to offer one's life for the jihad is incontrovertible evidence of one's purity and closeness to Allah.[18] The remainder of this chapter demonstrates that all of these jihadi tenets have become part and parcel of the CE's theo-ideology, behavior and aspirations.

The CE's Goals and Strategic Vision.

The ChRI's implicitly expanding pan-Caucasus ambitions became explicit and institutionalized in October 2007 with Dokku "Abu Usman" Umarov's declaration of the CE.[19] Umarov's declaration of the CE claimed not only domain over the entire North Caucasus from the Caspian to Black Seas, but it also included a declaration of jihad against the United States, Great Britain, Israel, and any country fighting Muslims anywhere on the globe.[20] The unilateral nature of this decision, although prompted and supported by both foreign jihadists and many North Caucasus mujahedin as well as by their Islamic texts, demonstrates the totalitarian essence of the Salafi takfirism. In order to achieve their local emirate, Umarov divided the Caucasus mujahedin into some five vilaiyats loosely based along the territorial borders of Russia's North Caucasus republics: the Nokchicho (Chechnya) Vilaiyat (NV), the Dagestan Vilaiyat (DV); the Galgaiche Vilaiyat (GV) covering Ingushetia and North Ossetiya; the United Vilaiyat of Kabardiya, Balkariya, and Karachai (OVKBK) covering the republics of Kabardino-Balkaria (KBR) and Karachaevo-Cherkessiya; and, the Nogai Steppe Vilaiyat (NSV) covering Krasnodar and Stavropol Krais. Except for the NSV, which has never been fully developed, each is headed by an amir with similar dictatorial powers. The chief theo-ideological figure is the vilaiyat's shariah court qadi. Qadis sometimes are amirs simultaneously.

In a May 2011 interview, Umarov again elaborated on the CE's expansive goals:

> We consider the CE and Russia as a single theater of war.
>
> We are not in a hurry. The path has been chosen, we know our tasks, and we will not turn back, Insha'Allah, from this path. Today, the battlefield is not just Chechnya and the Caucasus Emirate, but also the whole [of] Russia. The situation is visible to everybody who has eyes. The Jihad is spreading, steadily and inevitably, everywhere.
>
> I have already mentioned that all those artificial borders, administrative divisions, which the Taghut drew, mean nothing to us. The days when we wanted to secede and dreamed of building a small Chechen Kuwait in the Caucasus are over. Now, when you tell the young Mujahedeen about these stories, they are surprised and want to understand how those plans related to the Koran and the Sunnah.
>
> Alhamdulillah! I sometimes think that Allah has called these young people to the Jihad, so that we, the older generation, could not stray from the right path. Now we know that we should not be divided, and must unite with our brothers in faith. We must reconquer Astrakhan, Idel-Ural, Siberia — these are indigenous Muslim lands. And then, God willing, we shall deal with [the] Moscow District. [21]

The evidence of the CE's adoption of the global jihad's universal goals as its very own is overwhelming. Yet, most analysts and activists appear unaware or unwilling to acknowledge the fact.[22] Umarov has repeatedly associated the CE with the global jihad, from his announcement declaring the foundation of the CE and its jihad against anyone fighting against Muslims anywhere across the globe to his most recent February 2011 "Appeal to the Muslims of Egypt and Tunisia."[23] For example, in October 2010, Umarov addressed the global jihad:

> Today, I want to describe the situation in the world because, even if thousands of kilometers separate us, those mujahedin who are carrying out Jihad in Afghanistan, Pakistan, Kashmir and many, many other places, they are our brothers, and we today (with them) are insisting on the laws of Allah on this earth.

He also noted that the CE mujahedin follow the Afghani jihad closely by radio and Internet and that the Taliban are "opposed by Christian-Zionist forces led by America." In traditional jihadi fashion, Umarov calls jihadism's enemies "the army of Iblis" or the "army of Satan," uniting "the Americans, who today confess Christian Zionism, and European atheists, who do not confess any of the religions." Iblis fight so "there will be no abode for Islam (Dar as-Salam)" anywhere on earth.[24] A leading ideologist for the CE's Ingush mujahedin of its Galgaiche (Ingushetia) Vilaiyat, Abu-t-Tanvir Kavkazskii, laid out in detail the connection between the CE's prospective emirate and the grander global caliphate:

> In the near future we can assume that after the liberation of the Caucasus, Jihad will begin in Idel-Ural and Western Siberia. And, of course we will be obligated to assist with all our strength in the liberation of our brothers' lands from the centuries-long infidel yoke and in the establishment there of the laws of the Ruler of the Worlds. It is also possible that our help will be very much needed in Kazakhstan and Central Asia, and Allah has ordered us to render it. And we,

Allah willing, will destroy the laws of the infidel on the Central Asian lands in league with the mujahedin of Afghanistan. And it is impossible to forget our brothers in the Crimea, which is also land occupied by non-believers.[25]

The CE's top qadi has put it more explicitly and concisely: "We are doing everything possible to build the Caliphate and prepare the ground for this to the extent of our capabilities."[26]

Domestic Strategy.

The CE issues few documents indicating their strategy. However, some implicit strategic approaches can be sketched from some of its statements and propaganda articles. Essentially, the CE is attempting to create a revolutionary situation through the establishment of a credible, alternative claim on the sovereign right to rule in the North Caucasus and elsewhere in Russia. This state-building political strategy includes: (1) establishing a judicial system based on Shariah courts and qadis; (2) enforcement of Shariah law through attacks on owners, workers, and patrons of gaming, prostitution, drinking, and alcohol-selling establishments; (3) tax collection in the form of the Islamic tithe or *zakyat* to fund CE military, police, and judicial functions; and, (4) a more expanded propaganda strategy focused exclusively on proselytizing the Salafist theology and jihadist ideology by multiplying the number of CE-affiliated websites.[27] Military strategy compliments this political strategy, weakening the infidel state and regime by targeting state institutions, officials, and personnel—civilian, police, military, and intelligence alike.

Creating a credible alternative sovereignty requires not simply weakening local branches of the present Russian regime and state but also the federal government in Moscow and its affiliates across the federation. Combined with the basic homeland strategy focused on creating dual sovereignty in the Caucasus, there is an effort to expand operations and eventually more state-building efforts across Russia, using concentrations of Muslim populations in Tatarstan, Bashkortostan, and elsewhere as platforms from which the network could conceivably expand. Thus, CE amir Umarov promised to liberate not just Krasnodar Krai—part of its still very virtual Nogai Steppe Vilaiyat—but also Astrakhan and the entire Volga mega-region, which would include Tatarstan, Bashkortostan, and other predominantly Muslim Tatar-populated regions in Russia's Volga and Urals Federal Districts.[28] Simultaneously, attacks like those on the Nevskii Express St. Petersburg-Moscow train in November 2009, the Moscow subway system in March 2010, and Moscow's Domodedovo Airport in January 2011 serve the purpose of terrorizing the Russian elite and population, creating political disunity, and undermining the Russian will to fight for the region's continued inclusion in the federation.

Operational Capacity and Tactics.

Although the CE is overlooked by most terrorism or jihadism experts, its operational capacity puts the North Caucasus a distant third among the world's various jihadi fronts behind the Afghanistan-Pakistan (AfPak) theatre of AQ including the Taliban and their numerous allies in the region, and Yemen. In recent years, jihadi-related violence in the North Caucasus has outstripped that in Iraq. From late October 2007 through June 2011, CE mujahedin have carried out or been involved in approximately 1,800 attacks and violent incidents, with an increase in the number of attacks/incidents each full year of the CE's existence, 2008-10.[29] Those 1,800 attacks have killed approximately 1,300 and wounded 2,100 state agents (civilian officials and military, intelligence, and police officials and personnel) and killed 300 and wounded 800 civilians, for a total of some 4,500 casualties.[30] This amounts to nearly two attacks/incidents and more than three casualties per day. For comparison, for the period 2008-10, there were 1,527 U.S./North Atlantic Treaty Organization (NATO) troops killed and 9,703 U.S./NATO casualties in Afghanistan.[31]

Like its allies in the global jihadi revolutionary movement, the CE has carried out spectacular and horridly effective attacks, in particular tens of istishkhad operations—that is, suicide bombing operations. For example, in November 2009, the CE, perhaps its Riyadus Salikhiin Martyrs Brigade (RSMB), was behind the bombing of the Moscow-St. Petersburg Nevskii Express high speed train, which killed 21 and wounded 74 civilians. The explosion of the train was followed by a second as investigators arrived on the scene that slightly wounded several officials. In April 2009 amir Umarov announced after the CE's traditional spring planning shura that the CE had revived warlord and notorious terrorist Shamil Basaev's RSMB in 2008, and that it had already carried out two operations, including the November 2008 suicide bombing of a bus in Vladikavkaz, Ingushetia, that killed 14 and wounded 43 civilians.[32] In June 2009, the notorious ethnic Buryat-Russian Muslim convert Aleksandr Tikhomirov, a.k.a. Sheikh Said Abu Saad Buryatskii, masterminded the suicide bombing that severely wounded and nearly killed Ingushetia President Yunusbek Yevkurov and the August 2009 suicide bombing of the Ministry of Internal Affairs (MVD) district headquarters in Nazran that killed 24 MVD servicemen and wounded approximately 260 people, including 11 children, on the very day that Yevkurov returned to Ingushetia after months of hospitalization. Based with the CE's GV mujahedin and RSMB, Buryatskii wrote prolifically about the importance of istishkhad operations and his preparation with RSMB suicide bombers.[33] The equally notorious 'Seifullah Gubdenskii' Magomedali Vagabov, CE DV amir and CE qadi in 2010 until his demise in August of that year, organized the double suicide bombing of the Moscow Metropolitan subway in March 2010 that killed 40 and wounded 101 civilians, including some 10 traveling foreigners. (Both Buryatskii and Vagabov received Islamic education abroad before turning to jihad; the former — in Egypt, Yemen and perhaps Saudi Arabia; the latter in Pakistan.) On amir Umarov's orders, the CE's RSMB prepared and dispatched 20-year old Ingush Magomed Yevloev from Ingushetia to carry out the January 2011 suicide attack in the international terminal of Moscow's Domodedovo Airport that killed 37 and wounded 180.[34] In total, the CE has carried out some 36 suicide attacks since CE amir Umarov revived the RSMB: 1 in 2008, 16 in 2009, 14 in 2010, and 5 during the first 6 months of 2011. Istishkhad bombing operations are a distinct symptom of the CE's global jihadist theo-ideology and a symbol of its alliance with the global jihadi revolutionary movement.

THE CAUCASUS EMIRATE AND THE GLOBAL JIHADI REVOLUTIONARY MOVEMENT

The CE's jihadization of the Chechen and North Caucasus insurgency, in particular its alliance with the global jihadi revolutionary movement, imparts it strategic importance. The process of the Salafization of the ChRI's ranks was a long process and was driven by both the external influence of jihadist groups and the weak but nevertheless existing Salafist elements in the North Caucasus. The connections between AQ and the ChRI were common knowledge by the late 1990s among U.S. Government officials, intelligence analysts, and terrorism experts.[35] It was well-known and well-documented as early as the mid-1990s, for example, that the notorious Abu Ibn al-Khattab was an AQ operative and fought in the North Caucasus. The declassified Defense Intelligence Agency's (DIA) *Swift Knight Report* documents not just Khattab's deep involvement, but also that of AQ and Osama bin Laden personally with the ChRI in the mid-1990s.[36]

After the visit by Basaev and his ethnic Circassian or Akhaz fighters to Afghanistan, other radical nationalist and Sufi Chechen and Caucasus leaders followed with visits to bin Laden. An important but often overlooked DIA document details the results of some of those visits occurring in 1997. Thus, "several times in 1997 in Afghanistan bin Laden met with representatives of Movlady (Movladi) Udugov's party 'Islamic Way' (Islamskii Put') and representatives of Chechen and Dagestani Wahhabites from Gudermes, Grozny, and Karamakhi."[37] Udugov would become the chief ideologist and propagandist for both the ChRI and CE for a decade or more. The village of Karamakhi would be the locus of one of the self-declared Salafi

Islamic states that popped up intermittently in the late 1990s and the focal point of Khattab's, Basaev's, and Bagautdin's incursions and ultimate full-scale invasion of Dagestan in July and August 1999 that kicked off the second post-Soviet Russo-Chechen war. The result of this local-global nexus rooted in a common theo-ideology, mutual training camps, and overlapping personnel was a gradual but significant spread of Salafism and exclusionary takfirism among young Muslims across the Caucasus, creating an unprecedented recruitment pool for both the local and global jihads.

AQ and the Caucasus Islamic separatists agreed to create a jihadist movement and insurgency across Russia with AQ supplying funding, training, and fighters towards the goal of attacking Russians and Westerners. AQ money funded the establishment of training camps in Chechnya and Georgia's Pankisi Gorge, a steady supply of trainers for those camps, and fighters who spread out across Chechnya and the North Caucasus bringing the message of Salfism and global jihadism to the ChRI insurgents and their still very few allies in other North Caucasus regions such as the Republic of Dagestan and the Republic of Kabardino-Balkaria (KBR).[38] The DIA document details AQ's plans for the North Caucasus and Russia's Muslims:

> [R]adical Islamic (predominantly Sunni) regimes are to be established and supported everywhere possible, including Bosnia, Albania, Chechnya, Dagestan, the entire North Caucasus "from sea to sea", Central Asian republics, Tatarstan, Bashkortostan, all of Russia, Afghanistan, Pakistan, Turkey, Indonesia, Malaysia, Algeria, Morocco, Egypt, Tunisia, Sudan, and the states of the Persian Gulf. Terrorist activities are to be conducted against Americans and Westerners, Israe-

lis, Russians (predominantly Cossacks), Serbs, Chinese, Armenians, and disloyal Muslims. . . .

Special attention should be given to the Northern Caucasus, and especially Chechnya since they are regarded as areas unreachable by strikes from the West. The intent is to create a newly developed base for training terrorists. Amir Khattab and nine other militants of Usam Ben (sic) Laden were sent there with passports of Arab countries. They work as military instructors in Khattab's three schools; they also work as instructors in the army of Chechnya. Two more schools are being organized in Ingushetiya and Dagestan.[39]

"'Volunteers' from ben Laden's 'charity societies' from Pakistan and Afghanistan" went to Chechnya and the Northern Caucasus for a "new round of jihad against Cossacks and Russia."[40]

These AQ-affilitated "charity societies" ensured a steady flow of AQ funds, Salafist Wahhabi literature, and equipment to the region. The DIA's *Swift Knight Report,* as well as numerous trial transcripts, document the support rendered by the AQ-affiliated Benevolent International Foundation (BIF) and Al-Haramain to the ChRI or at least its radical wing beginning in the early 1990s.[41] The U.S. criminal prosecution of BIF for supporting terrorist activity reveals much about the AQ-BIF-ChRI connection. AQ used BIF for "the movement of money to fund its operations" and the support of "persons trying to obtain chemical and nuclear weapons on behalf of AQ," and BIF funded and supplied the Chechen separatist mujahedin before, during, and after the first Chechen-Russian war before Moscow forced BIF to shut down its operations in Russia.[42] AQ ruling Majlisul Shura member Seif al-Islam al-Masry was an officer in BIF's Grozny office, which moved to Ingushetia in 1998.[43] A BIF officer "had direct dealings with representatives of the Chechen mujahideen (guerrillas or freedom fighters) as well as Hezb i Islami, a military group operating in Afghanistan and Azerbaijan."[44] BIF's work with Hezb i Islami in Azerbaijan was likely related to AQ's corridor to the North Caucasus noted in the DIA document. BIF worked to provide the Chechen mujahedin with recruits, doctors, medicine, "money, an X-ray machine, and anti-mine boots, among other things."[45]

Beginning around 2000, the pro-Khattab and likely AQ-backed website, *Qoqaz.net* (Qoqaz is Arabic for Caucasus) sought funders and recruits for the Chechen jihad. *Qoqaz.net, Qoqaz.co.uk, Webstorage.com/~azzam,* and *Waaqiah.com* were created and supported by the AQ-affiliated Azzam Publications run by Babar Ahmad, both based in London. Azzam Publications produced numerous video discs featuring the terrorist attacks carried out by Khattab and Basaev as well as other ChRI operations.[46] According to the U.S. indictment of Ahmad, through Azzam he

> provided, through the creation and use of various internet websites, email communication, and other means, expert advice and assistance, communications equipment, military items, currency, monetary instruments, financial services, personnel designed to recruit and assist the Chechen Mujahideen and the Taliban, and raise funds for violent jihad in Afghanistan, Chechnya, and other places."

Azzam's web sites were created for communicating with: (1) "members of the Taliban, Chechen Mujahideen, and associated groups;" (2) others "who sought to support violent jihad" by providing "material support;" (3) individuals who wished to join these groups, "solicit donations," and arrange money transfers; and, (4) those who sought to purchase "videotapes depicting violent jihad in Chechnya, Bosnia, Afghanistan, and other lands of jihad, and the torture and killing of captured Russian troops." Videotapes, including those eulogizing dead fighters, were intended to help and indeed were used to solicit donations for the jihad in Chechnya and Afghanistan. Ahmad also assisted terrorists to secure temporary residence in London, and to travel to Afghanistan and Chechnya in order to participate in jihad. He also assisted terrorists in procuring "camouflage suits; global positioning system (GPS) equipment; and, other materials and information." Ahmad even put Shamil Basaev in touch with an individual who had traveled to the United States in order to raise money and purchase footwarmers for the ChRI fighters.[47]

Documents found in BIF's trash revealed that 42 percent of its budget was spent on Chechnya. During a 4-month period in 2000, BIF funneled $685,000 to Chechnya in 19 wire bank transfers through the Georgian Relief Association (GRA) in Tbilisi and various BIF accounts across the Commonwealth of Independent States (CIS), according to Citibank records introduced to the court. The GRA was actually a BIF front organization and was run by the brother of Chechen field commander Chamsoudin Avraligov, who was operating in AQ's training camp in Georgia's Pankisi Gorge.[48] Given that BIF was able to function in Russia for nearly a decade, claims made by Russian officials that AQ sent tens of millions of dollars to the North Caucasus mujahedin are plausible. One expert claims that AQ has funneled $25 million to the Chechen resistance including a one-time contribution in 2000 of $2 million, four Stinger missiles, 700 plastic explosive

packs amounting to over 350 kilograms, remote deto-
nators, and medical supplies.[49] Basaev acknowledged
in a 2004 interview receiving funds from international
Islamists "on a regular basis," perhaps understating
the amount he received that year at some $20 thou-
sand.[50] Despite the crackdown on Saudi-sponsored
and AQ-tied foundations like the BIF and the deaths
of Khattab in 2003 and Basaev in 2006, both the ChRI
and then its successor organization the CE continued
to receive foreign funding from Middle Eastern con-
tributions funneled through foreign and AQ-tied mujahedin through 2010.[51]

There were two principal figures involved in leading AQ's work in Chechnya and the North Caucasus:
Khattab, who turned high-ranking ChRI warlord and
Prime Minister Shamil Basaev to Salafi global jihadism
and together with him ran training camps and numerous operations, and Abu Sayif, who headed the Saudi
BIFs office in Grozny before the second war and ran
communications and the transport of supplies, fighters, and funding from AQ to the Caucasus. Upon ar-
riving in the Caucasus, Khattab linked up with Shamil
Basaev, a notorious terrorist in Chechnya, and married
the sister of Nadir Khachilaev, the leader of the Union
of the Muslims of Russia (*Soyuz musul'man Rossii*) and
an ethnic Lak from Dagestan.[52] By so cementing his
connection to a pan-Russian Islamist organization and
to Dagestan, Khattab was clearly using a standard AQ
approach of imbedding into the local social fabric in
the service of highjacking local Muslim nationalist and
Islamic movements for the global jihadi movement.

Excluding Khattab, AQ operative Abu Sayif, who
worked in the Chechen Foreign Ministry under Movladi Udugov in the inter-war years, played the most
important role in developing AQ's presence in Chech-

21

nya and the North Caucasus. Sayif coordinated the travel route, which was used to route volunteers and drug trafficking, and Sayif and Khattab were the only ones permitted to know the real names of the foreign volunteers. A travel route from Pakistan and Afghanistan to Chechnya, via Azerbaijan and Turkey, was established. The first group of some 25 "Afghan Arabs" arrived in Khattab's Vedeno camp in June 1998. Some were to pass through Tatarstan on their way to Central Asian Republics, where they were supposed to create "Wahhabite and Taliban cells, spreading terror against U.S., Russian, and other Western officials and businessmen."[53] It is now common knowledge that the lead perpetrator of the September 11, 2001 (9/11) attacks, Mohammed Atta, was on his way to Chechnya when he was sent to Germany and later the United States. Rohan Gunaratna claims that already by 1995, there were some 300 Afghan Arabs fighting in Chechnya against the Russians. They were joined by mujahedin from Bosnia and Azerbaidzhan.[54] Thus, there were perhaps as many as 500 foreign fighters in the North Caucasus on the eve of the Khattab-Basaev-led invasion of Dagestan. Indeed, the nexus of Dagestan, Karamakhi, bin Laden, and Khattab's and Basaev's Chechnya training camps draws a straight line from AQ in Afghanistan to the second post-Soviet Russo-Chechen war and the ChRI's expansion of operations across the North Caucasus.

Not only did AQ mujahedin fight in the North Caucasus during the ChRI struggle but North Caucasus mujahedin fought on other fronts in the global jihad during the same time frame. Two ethnic Kabardins from KBR were among eight ethnic Muslims from regions both in the North Caucasus and Volga area captured by U.S. forces in Afghanistan in 2001 fighting among the Taliban and AQ and sent to the Guantanamo Bay prison camp in 2002.[55] A brief official CE biography of late Dagestani amir and CE qadi Magomed Vagabov (a.k.a. Seifullah Gubdenskii) shows that in 2001-02 some members of his Gubden Jamaat went to Afghanistan after the rout of the joint Chechen-Dagestani-foreign jihadi force that invaded Dagestan in August 1999. Among those Gubden Jamaat members who went to Afghanistan was its then amir Khabibullah, who became the amir of "a Russian-speaking jamaat of AQ."[56] More recently, some members of the DV-tied cell, that was uncovered in the Czech Republic and discussed below, were at one time based in Germany and underwent training in Afghanistan and Pakistan.[57] We also know that the Tatar jihadi "Bulgar Jamaat," made up mostly of ethnic Tatars who made the hijra from Russia and now based in Waziristan, Pakistan, has declared jihad against Russia and stated that it includes "Dagestanis, Russians, Kabardins" and has carried out operations in Afghanistan.[58]

If one prefers to narrow the issue to Chechens, Bryan Glynn Williams claims that after extensive travel across Afghanistan, he was unable to find evidence that even one Chechen fighter ever fought there.[59] But there have been numerous reports of Chechens fighting not just in Afghanistan, but also in Iraq against U.S. forces.[60] In 2003, Indian police uncovered an AQ cell led by a Chechen planning to assassinate Vice Admiral V. J. Metzger, commander-in-chief of the U.S. Seventh Fleet, forcing the admiral's trip to India to be cancelled.[61] Every officer and junior officer with whom I have had the pleasure of speaking has claimed that he encountered a Chechen presence in both Afghanistan and Iraq. Almost all of these officers spoke some Russian. It is certainly true that some of these testimonials are cases of mistaken identity, taking Russian-speaking Central Asians for Chechens. But it simply strains credulity to believe that not a single Chechen has fought in Afghanistan, when we have seen that Americans, Germans, other Westerners, Central Asians, Tatars, Kabardins, and Dagestanis have been there.

These are a few examples of CE ties to other fronts in the global jihad. In the same month that the CE was formed (October 2007), the Lebanese government arrested four Russian citizens, including three ethnic North Caucasians (one from Dagestan), who were charged with belonging to Fatah-el-Islam, fighting in northern Lebanon that summer, and carrying out terrorist attacks against Lebanese servicemen while participating in an armed revolt in the Nahr el-Barid Palestinian refugee camp. Along with 16 Palestinians, they formed a Fatah cell.[62] According to a recent report by Russia's National Anti-Terrorism Committee, a Kabardin, who allegedly was recently fighting in Lebanon, returned home and was killed in Nalchik.[63]

Thus, there have been some, but very few Chechen or other North Caucasus mujahedin who have fought in Afghanistan, Iraq, and other fronts of the global jihad. The Chechen and then Caucasus mujahedin's operational connections with, and influence on the more central fronts of the global jihad are evident. However, these connections are less than robust and of limited strategic significance, with the caveat that a small number of well-funded and capable terrorists can do great damage, as we saw on 9/11. Neither the ChRI nor the CE ever declared themselves AQ in the Caucasus or North Caucasus. But the close ties that developed between the ChRI and AQ beginning in the inter-war period meant that the ChRI units and camps of foreign fighters and their local allies led by Khattab and Basaev became AQ's de facto, unofficial North Caucasus affiliate and a key, if relatively weak, front in the global jihad. The AQ-tied foreign fighters, many of whom settled down and even married in Chechnya and other North Caucasus republics after the second war, were in large part responsible for the growing influence of jihadist ideologies in the region and fundamentally altered the nature of what began as a secessionist struggle for Chechen independence; this is precisely what AQ had counted on when it infiltrated the ChRI.

AQ's intervention and the growing influence of the global jihadi revolutionary movement led the radical Chechen national separatist movement down a path traversed by many such movements across the Muslim world in recent decades. In the Caucasus, especially Dagestan, they mixed with the very limited indigenous history of Salfism and significant contemporary flood of young Caucasus Muslims to study abroad in the Middle East and South Asia, on the one hand, and of Wahhabi and other Salafi teachings from there to the Caucasus through the Internet on the other. In the 18th and certainly by the 19th centuries, Salafism was brought in from abroad by Caucasians like Mukhamad Al-Kuduki after travels in Egypt and Yemen introduced him to scholars like Salikh al-Yamani.[64] The revival of this relatively recent, if thin, Salafi Islamist usable past, along with the national myths during the *perestroika* and post-*perestroika* periods, yielded the rehabilitation and of the 19th century imams and religious teachers who led the *gazavats* against Russian rule teachers.[65] But the nationalist ideas and cadres were gradually displaced by jihadist elements, transforming the secular movement into a jihadist one. This process was increasingly legitimized and gained momentum as Islamic elements were incorporated into the ChRI proto-state and foreign Salafists, Wahabbis, and other Islamic extremists continued to infiltrate the movement throughout the 1990s and early 2000s, bringing finances, guerrilla and terrorist training and, most importantly, a new jihadist ideo-theological orientation. The Salafist historical myth and related historical figures served as models for some local Salafists, who played key roles in the ChRI's incomplete Islamization even before 2007.[66]

The combination of AQ and other foreign Salafi intervention, a usable indigenous Salafi historical myth, and locals studying Islam abroad influenced a small but highly motivated group of Islamist and ultimately jihadist leaders across the North Caucasus. Beginning in the early 1990s, thousands of Muslims from Russia traveled abroad to receive Islamic education in Islamic schools which were experiencing the rise of a significant global jihadi revolutionary movement. They returned home with Wahhabist and other forms of Salafist zeal for jihad and a strong sense of kinship with radical Islamists and mujahedin in Afghanistan, Lebanon, Iraq, and elsewhere. Three young, foreign-educated Muslims—"Sefullah" Anzor Astemirov, Sheikh Said Abu Saad Buryatskii (Aleksandr Tikhomirov), and "Seifullah Gubdenskii" Magomedali Vagabov—joined the ChRI's jihadi wing or later the CE and rose quickly up the CE's ranks, driving its expanding jihad on three main fronts outside Chechnya: Dagestan, Ingushetia, and KBR.

In the early 1990s, the foreign-educated Dagestani Salafist Ahmad-Kadi Akhtaev taught the first important post-Soviet Dagestani jihadi theo-ideologists, Magomed Tegaev and Bagautdin Magomedov (Kebedov), and the two leading ethnic Kabard jihadists, Musa Mukozhev and "Seifullah" Anzor Astemirov, both of whom studied abroad as well. Astemirov would play a key role in the formation of a small cadre of jihadi fighters in the KBR, in Umarov's decision to form the CE and jettison the ChRI Chechen nationalist project, and in the development of the CE's relationship with Jordanian Sheikh Maqdisi and thus the global jihadi revolutionary movement. In the mid-1990s, as one of the leading students at a madrassah run by the official Muslim Spiritual Administration (DUM) of the KBR, Astemirov was one among many sent by the DUM to study Islam abroad in an unknown higher education religious school in Saudi Arabia.[67] This set him and many other young Muslims from the KBR on the path of Islamism and ultimately jihadism.[68] In summer 2005 Mukozhev and Astemirov met with Basaev, and they agreed that they would transform their Islamist Jamaat of KBR into the ChRI North Caucasus Front's Kabardino-Balkaria Sector (KBS) on the condition that Sadulaev and Basaev saw through to the end the formation of a pan-Caucasus jihadi organization like the future CE based on a strict takfirist interpretation of Shariah law. In addition to this and his abovementioned role as CE qadi, Astemirov's organizational efforts as amir of the CE's OVKBK resulted in its becoming the CE's second most operationally active vilaiyat in 2010, ahead of Chechnya's NV and Ingushetia's GV.[69]

Sheikh Buryatskii is representative of an even more disturbing transformation which shows that one does not need to be a victim of Russian brutality and bad governance or the product of the Caucasus traditions of martial violence and blood revenge to join the

Caucasus jihad and that the jihadist theo-ideology is by itself a substantial driver of jihadism in the region. As his jihadi *nom de guerre* suggests, Buryatskii was part ethnic Buryat, a Mongol and traditionally Buddhist ethnic group, and part ethnic Russian. Born as Aleksandr Tikhomirov in 1982, he lived in far away Ulan-Ude, the capitol of Russia's republic of Buryatia. His mother was Russian and Orthodox Christian; his father was an ethnic Buryat and Buddhist.[70] Buryatskii studied at a Buddhist *datsan*, but at age 15 he converted to Islam. He moved to Moscow and then to Bugurslan, Orenburg where he studied at the Sunni madrasah, Rasul Akram. Buryatskii then studied Arabic at the Saudi-supported Fajr language center in 2002-05 before traveling to Egypt to study Islamic theology at Cairo's Al-Azhar University as well as under several authoritative sheikhs in Egypt, Kuwait and, according to Russian prosecutors, Saudi Arabia.[71] Buryatskii himself reveals what his education in the core of an umma plagued by global jihadi revolutionary ideology taught him:

> At one time when I was in Egypt at the lecture of one of the scholars, who openly said to us: "Do you really think that you can so simply spread the Allah's religion without the blood of martyrs?! The disciples of Allah's prophet spilt the blood of martyrs on many lands, and Islam bloomed on their blood!"[72]

Running afoul of the Egypt's secret services, Buryatskii returned to Russia.[73] Buryatskii left for the Caucasus jihad in May 2008.[74]

Assigned by Umarov to the CE's GV in Ingushetia, the fervent Buryatskii became a recruiting draw. In 2009, Buryatskii was the CE's main, if fatal, attraction and its most effective propagandist and operative, showing shades of the charisma and ruthlessness for which Shamil Basaev became infamous. His articles detailing his mentoring of RSMB suicide bombers and his video lectures propagandizing jihadism and the importance of istshkhad drew new forces to the CE's once relatively quiet Ingush mujahedin. Buryatskii's activity was perhaps the main factor making the CE's GV the most operationally capacious of its vilaiyats in 2008-09, leading in the number of attacks both years.[75] Thus, there is a direct line between Buryatskii's Islamic conversion and study abroad to the explosion of terrorism in Ingushetia during 2008-09. Buryatskii is but one of several ethnic Russian and Slavic converts to Islam from outside Russia's Muslim republics who have become prominent CE terrorists in recent years, including Pavel Kosolapov, Vitalii Razdobudko, Maria Khorsheva, and Viktor Dvorakovskii.[76]

In contrast to Astemirov and Buryatskii, Vagabov was influenced by Pakistani Salafism. After studying Islam locally in Dagestan, he began to work with missionaries of the peaceful Pakistan-based international Salafist sect Tabligh Jamaat in Dagestan. His native Gubden District was declared the Tablighists' center for the call to the Tabligh in Russia. Vagabov then traveled in 1994 to Raiwand, Pakistan, the center of the Tabligh Jamaat movement, and studied there for several months in a madrassah learning the Koran by heart and receiving the diploma of a *khafiz*. Traveling on to Karachi, he studied the fundamentals of Shariah law apparently both at university and privately with sheikhs and became an adherent of Salafism and the writings of imam Abul Hasan Al-Ashari, Al-Ibana, and Risalyatu ila Aglyu Sagr-Vibabil Abvab. Vagabov returned home in 1997, opened the School of Khafiz in Gubden to courses on the hadiths, and traveled to

Chechnya where he met with Khattab and underwent military training in the AQ-funded camps. He fought for the Salafis, who declared an independent Islamic state in Karamakhi and two other Dagestani villages in 1998, and in the 1999 Khattab-Basaev invasion of Dagestan that kicked off the second Chechen war.[77] In the 2000s, Vagabov rose up the ranks of the ChRI's Dagestani Front and then the CE's DV. He played a lead role in building up the DV's dominant Central Sector, which has made Dagestan the locus of the highest number of attacks of any Russian region since April 2010. Vagabov also organized the pivotal March 2010 Moscow subway suicide bombings carried out by the respective wives of his predecessor and successor as DV amir. In June 2010, Umarov appointed him as the DV's amir, and Astemirov's successor as the CE's qadi.[78] Vagabov's biography draws a direct line from the umma's global jihadi revolutionary movement and radical Pakistani madrassahs, mosques, and universities to the rise of the Dagestani jihad within the overall CE and to terrorism in Moscow itself with the Moscow subway bombing among others. Although Astemirov, Vagabov, and Buryatskii were killed in 2010, by then each had left their mark on the CE's expansion across the Caucasus and transformation into a viable jihadist project allied with the global jihadi revolutionary alliance inspired by AQ and its takfirist theo-ideology.

As AQ and the global jihadi revolutionary alliance have evolved into a more decentralized network of jihadi groups, interacting increasingly for theo-ideological sustenance, funding, training, and operational planning through the Internet rather than directly, the CE integrated into the AQ's wider network of jihadi websites. In this way, it developed relationships with jihadi leaders and philosophers such as

Maqdisi, mentioned earlier, and AQ in the Arabian Peninsula (AQAP) and Anwar Al-Awlaki. The AQ-affiliated website, *Ansar al-Mujahideen* (*www.ansar1.info/*), is used to recruit fighters and raise funds for the CE by those involved in the Belgian plot uncovered last autumn and is closely linked to AQ. The *Ansar al-Mujahideen* network is typically regarded as a self-started jihadi and pro-AQ site that helps propagandize and recruit for the global jihad and AQ.[79] *Ansar al Mujahideen's* English-language forum's (AMEF) leading personality was "Abu Risaas" Samir Khan until mid-2010 when he turned up working with Awlaki in AQAP.[80] The Virginian Zachary Adam Chasser, alias Abu Talhah al-Amriki, in prison for assisting the Somalian AQ affiliate Al-Shabaab, also participated in AMEF.[81] *Ansar al Mujahideen's* German-language sister site is closely associated with the Global Islamic Media Front (GIMF), which also has produced several operatives arrested for involvement in AQ terrorism plots.[82] The Taliban has authorized the *Ansar al-Mujahideen* network as one of three entities that may publish its official statements, and *Ansar al-Mujahideen's* founder noted "we have brothers from Chechnya and Dagestan."[83]

In December 2010, *Ansar al-Mujahideen* announced "the Start of a New Campaign in Support of the Caucasus Emirate," signaling a request for fighters and funds for the CE and emphasizing: "We ask Allah to make this year a year of constant discord and increasing enmity for the enemies of the Islamic Emirate of the Caucasus." The announcement welcomed emerging signs of jihadism in Tatarstan and Bashkortostan, asking Allah for "a new generation of scholars" to replace Astemirov, Buryatskii, and AQ operative Omar al-Sayif, all mentioned by name.[84] *Ansar al-Mujahedeen* soon partnered with Astemirov's and the CE OVKBK's *Islamdin.com* to create a new Russian-language global jihadi website (*al-ansar.info*) no later than July 2010.[85] In August, the webmaster of *Ansar al-Mujahideen*, an ethnic Moroccan named Faisal Errai, was arrested in Spain. Spanish authorities also reported that the website was already raising money for terrorists in Chechnya and Afghanistan.[86] The Russian-language *Al-Ansar.info* was set up to "highlight news summaries of the Jihad on all fronts, both in the Caucasus and in all other lands of the fight" and publish old and new works of scholars of the "ahli sunny ual' jama'a." The fact that it contains primarily Russian-language but also English-language content suggests, along with other factors, that AQAP's Awlaki may be a driving force behind the *Ansar al-Mujahideen* network of which *Al-Ansar.info* is a part. Thus, *Islamdin.com*'s announcement of the joint project with the *Ansar al-Mujahideen* network extensively quotes Awlaki (who otherwise retains a high profile on CE sites) on the value of being a "jihadist of the internet."[87] *Islamdin.com* posted the first part of Awlaki's Al-Janna the day after this announcement, and CE websites continue to post Awlaki's works.[88] With the CE tied into the global jihadi revolutionary alliance and once again plugged into the AQ-affiliated Internet network, it was just a matter of time before it developed a more international role.

DOMESTIC AND INTERNATIONAL SECURITY IMPLICATIONS

The CE's more expansive aspirations and growing ties with the global jihad revolutionary movement have been accompanied by closer propaganda and operational ties to jihadists in other regions of Russia, the former Soviet Union, other fronts in the global jihad and, per Maqdisi's call, even Europe. Moreover, there are even broader strategic implications impinging on both international and U.S. national security.

To the Volga and Beyond.

Aside from the abovementioned train, subway, and airport attacks in and around Moscow, the CE is involved in several projects inside Russia far beyond the virtual emirate's supposed borders. But the CE also has plans to expand operations beyond Russia. Already in January 2006, Basaev warned that by summer, the ChRI's combat jamaat network would "cross the Volga," suggesting expansion to Tatarstan, Bashkortostan, and likely beyond.[89] In June 2006, then ChRI amir Umarov issued a decree creating Volga and Urals Fronts, hoping to expand operations to Tatarstan, Bashkortostan, and other ethnic Tatar and Bashkir communities across Russia.[90] Through 2009 there was much CE propaganda targeting Tatars and Bashkirs but few jihadi deeds. A group called Islamic Jamaat was uncovered in 2007, but there was no evidence that it had CE ties.[91] Rather, the group may have been the predecessor of the allegedly CE-tied so-called Oktyabrskii Jamaat uncovered in 2010, both of which could have been connected to the so-called Uighur-Bulgar Jamaat (UBJ), which may be one and the same as the abovementioned Bulgar Jamaat, fighting with the Taliban and al-Qaeda in Afghanistan and Pakistan.[92] The UBJ, like the Bulgar Jamaat, is Tatar-dominated and adheres to the ideology of resettling in order to fight the infidel (at-Takfir Val Khidzhra). Several alleged operatives from the UBJ were arrested in Bashkortostan in August 2008 after a shootout with

Bashkir police in Salavat, Bashkortostan. They went on trial in April 2009 for allegedly planning terrorist attacks in the republic. According to Bashkir authorities, the UBJ was founded by Bashkiriya native Pavel Dorokhov, who underwent training in al-Qaeda and Taliban camps.[93]

More recently, during 2010 and early 2011, several arrests of alleged mujahedin with ties to the CE have been made and the first apparent jihadi attacks occurred in Tatarstan, Bashkortostan, and Astrakhan.[94] This suggests that the CE may indeed be expanding operations to these key Muslim communities. In addition, this past winter a group from Tatarstan and/or Bashkortostan appealed to Umarov to recognize their self-declared Idel-Ural Vilaiyat (IUV) and provide financial and other assistance in setting up training camps in the southern Ural Mountains and in organizing attacks.[95] As of mid-summer 2011, there had been no public response by Umarov, though clandestine assistance cannot be ruled out. The UBJ/Bulgar Jamaat also could be playing a role in these possible efforts by these Tatars and Bashkirs. Bringing Tatarstan, Bashkortostan, and Astrakhan would help form a bridgehead to Siberia, the Far East, and Central Asia. Gaining a foothold in ethnic Bashkir and especially Tatar communities in these regions would vastly expand the CE's pool of potential recruits and geographical reach into both Russia and Central Asia, since Tatar communities can be found in almost all of Russia's provincial capitals, including Moscow and St. Petersburg, and in Central Asia. Expansion along these lines would further tax Russian resources, already burdened by massive federal subsidies to the North Caucasus. Although it is unlikely that the CE will achieve substantial progress in expanding to a permanent presence in the Volga, Urals, or Siberian regions, the ChRI's and CE's record in expanding operations across the North Caucasus argues against complacency. Few expected that Ingushetia rather than Chechnya would be the center of gravity of the jihadi in 2008 and 2009, or that Dagestan and KBR would supersede both Vainakh republics in the number of jihadi operations in 2010. Even a small IUV enterprise could significantly complicate Moscow's coordination problems, given some creativity and modest resources on the part of the mujahedin.

More disturbing is the threat posed by the CE mujahedin to the 2014 Olympic Games to be held in the North Caucasus resort city of Sochi, Krasnodar. The area comes under the CE's NSV, which is responsible for Russia's Krasnodar and Stavropol regions but it has not demonstrated much of an existence no less capacity, with a caveat: Recent suicide operations, failed and successful, have involved ethnic Russian Islamic converts from Stavropol. The advantage that less conspicuous ethnic Russian mujahedin might offer in an operation targeting Sochi raises red flags. These same ethnic Russian mujahedin's ties to the most capacious of the CE's vilaiyats, the DV, raise more concerns.[96] Not only have the Dagestani mujahedin carried out the highest number of operations each month since April 2011, but the DV has also led in the number of suicide bombings and created its own Riyadus Salikhiin Jamaat (RSJ).[97] In August 2010, Dagestani mujahedin issued an explicit promise of "operations in Sochi and across Russia and more 'surprises' from the horror of which you will blacken."[98] The CE's OVKBK mujahedin also might be involved in an attack on the Sochi Games. Its field of operations, the republics of KBR and lesser so Karachaevo-Cherkessiya (KChR), are geographically closer to Sochi than is Dagestan.[99] In February 2011, the OVKBK carried out a series coordinated attacks against the winter ski resort area around Mt. Elbrus. The entire operation resembled a training operation for an attack on Sochi, and the OVKBK warned it would continue to fight infidel Russian development efforts and international culture in the region.[100] Thus, CE plans for Sochi could include a joint DV-OVKBK operation or separate ones by the DV and OVKBK with built-in redundancy, utilizing ethnic Russian suicide bombers. The possibility that the CE might strike at the Sochi Games, an international target, is strengthened by its active support for the global jihadi revolutionary alliance's goals.

The Eurasian Horizon.

There already are connections between the CE and other post-Soviet jihadists. At the most general level, mujahedin from Central Asian states, Azerbaijan, and even Georgia, have turned up among the CE mujahedin, but the reverse has not been true, putting aside the CE's use of Georgia's Pankisi Gorge as a rear base. The CE has declared not only all Muslim lands in Russia, but also the entire Caucasus as its rightful domain.[101] In the Caucasus writ large, Azerbaijan, bordering and having some ethnic and Islamic overlap with Dagestan, the present spearhead of the CE's activity, is most vulnerable to CE penetration. Its Islamic population includes nationalities such as the Lezgins, who straddle the Azerbaijani-Dagestan border and are an important nationality in Dagestan. As noted above, the ChRI, AQ, and its affiliated charity societies used Azerbaijan as a transit point for funneling funds, cadres, and weapons to Chechnya in the 1990s. The CE also seems to be taking note. Recent incursions south by likely CE mujahedin into northern Azerbaijan as well as jihadist activity in Baku suggest mujahedin could threaten this strategically important state.[102] Recently, the DV added an Azerbaijan Jamaat with unidentified locale and goals.[103] The CE's capacious vanguard DV puts Umarov within striking range of international and U.S. interests in Azerbaijan such as oil company headquarters, refineries, and the Baku-Tbilisi-Ceyhan pipeline carrying oil to Europe. Clearly, a CE or other significant jihadi presence in Azerbaijan would have security implications for the entire Transcaucasus and the Persian Gulf region.

The bad blood between Moscow and Tbilisi created by the 2008 Georgian-Russian 5-day war is beginning to influence the situation in the North Caucasus. To be sure, there is little evidence of the ethno-nationalist mobilizational effect on Russia's Circassian nationalities that many predicted would be a result of Russia's recognition of the independence of Abkhazia. However, Georgia has been speculating on the situation in the region, especially the Circassian genocide issue, as the Sochi Olympics approach. It has opened up a television and radio company that broadcasts propaganda to the region, waived visa requirements for North Caucasus residents, and adopted a parliamentary resolution calling for a boycott of the Sochi Olympics and Russian and international recognition of the Russians' rout and partially forced exile of Circassians in the 1860s as a genocide. Some Georgian opposition figures and one former U.S. official claim that President Mikheil Saakashvili's government is providing financial and training assistance to the CE.[104] Georgia's policies could radicalize some Circassians and thus improve the CE OVKBK's and NSV's prospects for recruitment.

Consistent with the interrelated goals of recreating the caliphate and extending the CE through the Volga and southern Urals regions as a bridge to Central Asia, the CE maintains relations with Central Asian jihadi organizations tied to AQ and the Taliban in AfPak such as the Islamic Movement of Uzbekistan (IMU) and the IMU splinter group, the Islamic Jihad Union (IJU). Both the IMU and IJU have fighters in Afghanistan, train in Pakistan, and fight in both as well as in Central Asia. In a May 2007 statement, IJU amir Ebu Yahya Muhammad Fatih stated that the IJU had "also been working on our common targets together with Caucasian mujahedeens."[105] In March 2011, the IJU's media department, Badr At-Tawhid, sent a 7-minute video message to the CE mujahedin from the IJU's amirs in the "land of Horosan," Afghanistan.[106] It praised the CE mujahedin for joining the global jihad and noted: "In our jamaat, there are many brothers who were trained or fought on the lands of the Caucasus Emirate."[107] The CE DV cell uncovered in the Czech Republic discussed below could have been training with the IJU or IMU. CE websites regularly cover and provide at least propaganda support to Central Asia's leading jihadi organizations, including the IMU and IJU. Thus, the CE reported extensively on the series of suicide, improvised explosive devices (IEDs), and ambush attacks and skirmishes carried out by the IMU, IJU, and/or a possible subunit thereof, the "Jamaat 'Ansarullah' in Tajikistan," during autumn 2010 in Hujand, Sogdo Oblast' and elsewhere in Tajikistan.[108]

The CE Ingush GV's website *Hunafa.com*, founded by Buryatskii, has shown a special interest in the emergence of jihadism in Kazakhstan, carrying propaganda materials from a Kazakhstan jihadi jamaat "Ansaru-d-din," calling Kazakhstan's Muslims to jihad and a fatwa issued by Sheikh Abul-Mundhir Al-Shinkiti, asserting the Shariah legality of attacking police and fighting jihad in Kazkahstan, even though the Muslims there are weak and small in number.[109] It is unclear whether the CE, GV independently, or Absaru-d-din played a role in recent bombings and attacks on police this year.[110] The CE's main website *Kavkaz tsentr* also reported in March 2011 the bayat to the Islamic Emirate of Afghanistan, Mullah Muhammad Omar Mujahid, the Islamic group taken by a group of Kyrgyzstan mujahedin, Jaish Jamaat al-Mahdi (Amir-ul-Mu'minin), and their call to the Kyrgyz to take up jihad.[111]

Thinking Globally: The CE and Jihad in Europe.

The CE's rabid anti-infidelism is not new; the ChRI's websites were replete with anti-Western, anti-Semitic, and anti-American articulations as far back as 2005.[112] The CE's growing ties with AQ and the global jihadi revolutionary alliance produced in 2010 what appears to have been the first CE-tied activity in Europe: the plot by "Shariah4Belgium" broken up in November 2010, and the DV-tied Czech cell uncovered in April 2011. On November 23, 11 suspects tied to the jihadi Shariah4Belgium group were arrested in Belgium, the Netherlands, Germany, Spain, Morocco, and Saudi Arabia on suspicion of planning terrorist attacks in Belgium, recruiting "jihadist candidates" and financing the CE. Earlier in 2010, Shariah4Belgium leader Abou Imran declared that the White House would "be conquered," and "Europe will be dominated by Islam."[113] The Belgian-based detainees included six Moroccan Belgian citizens detained in Antwerp, three Moroccan Belgian citizens arrested in the Netherlands, and two

Chechens apprehended in the German city of Aachen near the Belgian border[114] All the suspects held dual citizenship and belonged to the Antwerp-based Shariah4Belgium.[115] Belgian police said the Shariah4Belgium cell had ties to a local Islamic Center and had been under investigation since at least 2009. One of the Russian nationals was a 31-year-old "Chechen" arrested in Aachen, Germany, under a European arrest warrant issued by Belgium who was suspected of having recruited young people to fight in Chechnya. All the detainees, including the two Chechens, were said to have been involved in both recruiting and financing for the CE and planning attacks in Belgium[116] A third Chechen supporter of Doku Umarov allegedly involved in the Shariah4Belgium plot was arrested on December 1 at Vienna's Schwechat airport on the basis of one of nine international arrest warrants issued by the Belgian government.[117] The 32-year old Aslambek I., as he was identified by the authorities, was detained upon his return from the hajj to Mecca in connection with an international plot to attack "a NATO facility in Belgium."[118] Aslambek I. reportedly lived in the Austrian town of Neunkirchen with this family and was planning to bomb a train carrying NATO troops. Earlier, he reportedly lost both his hands in a grenade attack in Chechnya and had been arrested in Sweden for smuggling weapons, was released, and then left for Mecca[119]

It remains unclear whether this CE-connected plot was part of the reported AQ plan to carry out a series of Christmas terrorist attacks in the United States and Europe last holiday season.[120] Besides the Chechen origins of three members of the Belguim4Shariah cell and their assistance to the CE, there was other evidence of the plot's connection simultaneously to the CE,

AQ, and the global jihad. On June 20, the OVKBK's *Islamdin.com* posted an appeal from Belgian Muslims to Maqdisi, underscoring once again the way in which the CE's tie to Maqdisi unites it with the larger global jihadi revolution.[121] More significantly, the arrested Shariah4Belgium suspects were said to have been using the jihadi website *Ansar al-Mujahidin* in carrying out their activity.[122] As noted above, the CE OVKBK's *Islamdin.com* co-sponsored with *Ansar al-Mujahidin* the Russian-language forum *Al-Ansar.info*.

In April 2011, counterterrorism officials in the Czech Republic uncovered an international cell in Bohemia connected to the CE's DV. According to the chief of the Czech Unit for Combating Organized Crime (UOOZ) Robert Slachta, the group included one Chechen, two or three Dagestanis, two or three Moldovans, and two Bulgarians, who are accused variously of weapons possession, document falsification, financing and supplying terrorist organizations, specifically the DV's new members, with weapons and explosives.[123] Documents relating to the Dagestan mujahedin in both Arabic and Russian were found during the arrests. The apartment of the Chechen involved in the Czech cell was reported to have contained significant quantities of arms and ammunition. Six of the eight accused were arrested in the Czech Republic, with two members still at large in Germany. There was also an unidentified ninth member. Profits made from the falsification of passports and other documents were sent to Dagestan as were weapons and explosives purchased by the cell. None of those arrested were suspected of planning terrorist attacks in the Czech Republic.[124] However, one press report claimed that the Bulgarian members of the group were involved in planning terrorist attacks in unidentified other states.[125] In June 2011, two more unidentified Russian citizens were arrested in Germany engaging in the same activity for the DV and perhaps working with the abovementioned DV Czech cell.[126] The CE- and DV-tied Czech Republic cell represents global jihadi thinking and suggests the CE and its DV as clear and present dangers to the Sochi Games.

On July 5, 2010, French police and security carried out a counterterrorism operation arresting five Chechens, three men aged 21 to 36, and two women, in several districts across the city of Le Mans. One of the three males was described as an imam and father of five. Reportedly, French counterterrorism was tipped off by Russian security after they arrested a Chechen citizen in Moscow in possession of weapons, explosives, plans for making bombs, and a residence permit issued by France's Prefecture de la Sarthe. Russian investigators also discovered that the wife of the arrested Chechen lives in Le Mans. The three males were arraigned on July 9 and charged on suspicion of "criminal association in relation with a terrorist enterprise."[127] The CE also could be connected directly or indirectly to several Chechens arrested individually in Europe in recent years; for example Lors Doukaev, who was sentenced in May 2011 to 12 years in prison for planning an attack on the offices of the newspaper *Jyllands-Posten*, which published the famous 12 caricatures of the Prophet Mohammad in 2005.[128] In sum, the CE and perhaps lone wolf terrorists inspired by it are posing a new threat to Europe and the West.

Potential Threats to U.S. Interests.

The CE also poses a potential threat to U.S. interests and citizens, if not the homeland. It may be significant that both the Nevskii Express and Domodedovo Airport attacks targeted transport infrastructure where foreigners, in particular Americans, are often present. The potential threat to U.S. interests and even personnel is suggested by the Nevskii Express attack. The Moscow-St. Petersburg rail route is located within 100 miles of the northern stretch of the Northern Distribution Route (NDR) supplying U.S. and NATO troops in Afghanistan. Beginning in Latvia, it traverses through northeast Russia on its way to Central Asia and Afghanistan. If the Shariah4Belgium plot was intended to target NATO transport, then a similar project to one that would target the NDR has already been on the CE-tied jihadists' agenda. Finally, aside from the numerous propaganda attacks on the U.S. extant on CE websites, in 2010 two sites taken together thrice published the infamous al-Fahd fatwa calling for the use of weapons of mass destruction (WMD) against the Americans.[129] To be sure, in contrast to the ChRI, there is only limited evidence to suggest that CE operatives intend or have attempted to acquire chemical, biological, radiological, or nuclear materials.[130] However, the CE's jihadization and the al-Fahd posting suggest a theo-ideological orientation that could so incline CE operatives to employ such tactics, and Russian Federal Security Service (FSB) Director Aleksandr Bortnikov's claim in June 2010 that terrorists continue to "attempt to acquire nuclear, biological, and chemical components" across the former Union of Soviet Socialist Republics (USSR) underscores the point.[131]

RUSSIAN COUNTER-JIHADISM POLICY

How is Moscow dealing with the CE insurgency and its alliance with the global jihad? It must be noted that the derision that many in the West devoted to Russian President Vladimir Putin's claims that Russia was dealing with international terrorism was misplaced. Putin was exaggerating his claim but not inventing it out of whole cloth, as the discussion above of AQ's ties to those ChRI elements involved in the 1999 invasion of Dagestan clearly shows. There is probably some truth to the assumption that Putin's claim was intended to serve as a justification for Russia's heavy-handed tactics in dealing with the ChRI and CE. Russian military, police, and special security forces have committed and, to a much lesser degree, continue to commit atrocities. However, the last few years have seen a considerable shift in the Russian strategy and tactics to include more elements of soft power in its overlapping counterinsurgency and counterterrorism, including attempts to combat jihadism theo-ideologically and through greater investment in the socioeconomic development of the North Caucasus.

Federal Policy.

Already during Putin's second term, there was a shift to include nonmilitary means: (1) better intelligence gathering and dissemination and better inter-operational coordination among the siloviki with the creation of federal and regional anti-terrorism committees for searching out and destroying CE amirs and operatives; (2) the removal from office of the oldest, longest-serving, and most odious of the North Caucasus republics' presidents, with the exception of

Chechenya's Ramzan Kadyrov and Ingushetia's Murat Zyazikov; and, (3) "draining the pond" of mujahedin through a fourth amnesty in 2006 which brought in 600 mujahedin from the forest.[132] Russian security and local police forces have become quite efficient at eliminating top CE leaders, with the exception of CE amir Umarov.[133] On June 9, 2009, the FSB managed for the first time to capture rather than kill a major CE amir, the CE's military amir, and the CE GV's amir and vali "Magas" Ali Taziyev (a.k.a. Akhmed Yevloyev). His capture likely led to actionable intelligence that has facilitated many of the increasing number of CE amirs killed since then. Also during his second term, Putin undertook a massive reconstruction effort for Chechnya, which after years of slow progress finally achieved considerable results. Groznyi has been almost completely rebuilt, and Chechnya's second city, Gudermes, is also making progress. The reconstruction efforts provided some employment for Chechen youth, but unemployment remains high, and Kadyrov has been criticized for funneling work to his Benoi and political clans. Putin-era anti-extremism laws remain in force and far too broad, allowing Ministry of Internal Affairs (MVD) and FSB operatives to apply them occasionally against journalists, moderate Muslims, and certain Islamic texts.

Under the Medvdev presidency, Russia has moved further in complimenting hard power with a robust soft power component in attempting to tackle jihadism in the Caucasus. In his first annual presidential address to Russia's Federal Assembly in November 2009, President Dmitry Medvedev called the North Caucasus Russia's "most serious domestic political problem" and announced a federal program to invest 800 billion rubles in Ingushetia, which since the summer of 2007 had been the center of gravity of the jihad, with the largest number of CE attacks of any North Caucasus region.[134] Medvedev also fired the extremely unpopular, incompetent, and violence-prone Ingushetiyan president Murat Zyazikov, who, largely on the strength of his FSB career, had been ensconced in power by Putin through a series of electoral manipulations. Under Zyazikov, Ingushetia saw abductions skyrocket, with many suspecting Zyazikov's cousin, who headed the security forces, of organizing the abductions. The final straw for Zyazikov came when Ingushetia's top opposition leader Magomed Yevloyev was shot while in the custody of the Ingushetia's MVD chief, after arguing with Zyazikov on a plane flight in August 2008. Zyazikov's removal and the security forces' killing of Buryatskii and GV amir Taziyev were followed since March 2010 by a fall both in attacks by the CE and abductions in the republic. Medvedev's federal assistance program for Ingushetia has made it since 2009 the most highly subsidized region in Russia, with 91 percent of the republic's budget being federally funded. From 2008 to 2010, expenditures increased for sectors crucial to socioeconomic development and jobs: by 282 percent for housing, 110 percent for economic development, 103 percent for education, with slightly lower increases for state agency expenditures, culture, health, and sport.[135]

Medvedev also moved to increase, better target, and ensure proper use of funding for the North Caucasus as a whole by creating the North Caucasus Federal District (SKFO) and appointing as its presidential envoy and as federal government deputy premier, the former businessman and Krasoyarsk Governor Aleksandr Khloponin. It is planned to fold the federal targeted programs for the North Caucasus, Chechnya, and Ingushetia into a single program, with one-third of the unified program designated for the most jihad-plagued republic, Dagestan.[136] Medvedev's June 2011 proposal to decentralize aspects of government to the regions and municipalities appears to be dictated in part by the situation in the North Caucasus, as SKFO envoy Khloponin has been assigned to draft the details for the decentralization of interbudgetary relations along with his fellow vice premier Dmitrii Kozak.[137] Since 2008, federal expenditures have increased in all the SKFO's regions, except for Chechnya. This has led to some modest economic growth for the SKFO as a whole, with some republics' economic growth outpacing the federal average. However, unemployment remains high, especially youth unemployment.[138]

In line with Medvedev's overall liberalization policies and his turn to more use of soft power in the North Caucasus, Prime Minister Putin announced a radical departure in Kremlin policy in the Caucasus, unveiling an ambitious economic development program for the region that was long overdue. He also called for the North Caucasus governments to open up in order to attract private investment, to pay more attention to the views of human rights activists, to encourage the development of civil society, and to air more federal broadcasts offering "objective and honest stories about life in the North Caucasus" and not an "artificially" drawn "soft and pleasing picture." The new development strategy detailed in Putin's speech is to integrate the North Caucasus into the Russian and global economies and to create 400,000 new jobs in the region by 2020 by: (1) plugging the region into the international North-South transit corridor linking Russia and Europe with Central Asian and Gulf states; (2) organizing several major public works and construction projects toward that end, to include building a major oil refinery in Chechnya's capital; (3) creating a modern tourism industry including a system of ski and other recreational resorts; and, (4) increasing North Caucasians' access to university education.[139]

Specifically, these goals are to be achieved by building a network of highways, renovating airports, and developing energy projects and recreation resort areas across the region. The construction and resulting resort-related businesses will help solve the region's unemployment problem. The government is already constructing highways around and between cities such as Mozdok in Republic of Ingushetia, Nalchik (the capital of the KBR), and Stavropol (capital of Stavropol Krai or Territory). A highway is being designed for Chechnya's second largest city, Gudermes, and another for Beslan, North Ossetia, will be commissioned by 2015. Another approximately 150-kilometer highway will link Cherkassk with Sukhum, the capital of Georgia's breakaway republic of Abkhazia, through a six-kilometer tunnel to be constructed through the mountains. The airports in Magas (Ingushetia), Beslan, and Stavropol's Shpakovskoye and Mineralny Vody airports will be modernized. In the field of energy, he announced new hydroelectricity projects for the mountainous region and the construction of a Rosneft oil refinery in Chechnya's capital, Grozny, to be commissioned in 2014. The total sum of investments for these anticipated economic projects will be 3.4 trillion rubles, according to Putin. The government is ready to cover risk for private investors guaranteeing up to 70 percent of project costs. The government will choose investors and distribute money through a new North Caucasian branch of Russia's Development Bank. This year, three federal programs—one for the entire region and one each for Chechnya and Ingushetia—will invest 20 billion rubles (some $700 million) in social and economic development projects in the North Caucasus. Putin also announced plans to develop the education infrastructure in the North Caucasus. A new proposal is to require that Russia's leading universities admit 1,300 students from North Caucasian republics annually. A project to build one of the eight federal universities in the North Caucasian District was announced in January.[140]

Putin also proposed "alpine skiing, ethnographic, or family" tourism. Specifically, he proposed creating a network of ski resorts across the region stretching from the Caspian to Black Seas building on the Elbrus ski resort in KBR. Mt. Elbrus is the highest mountain in Europe. This resort area was targeted by the OVKBK in February 2011, which issued an explicit statement that it would fight to prevent any resort development and keep out Russian and foreign infidel influence.[141] The planned tourism cluster will include resorts in Dagestan, North Ossetia, KBR, Karachaevo-Cherkessiya and Adygeya. The resorts should accommodate 100,000 tourists and create 160,000 jobs. Putin also announced plans to upgrade the Mineralnyi Vody hot springs and spa resort in Stavropol into a "hi-tech resort" and the nucleus of the healthcare and tourism industries of the region. He promised eight billion rubles in investments to kick start the tourism industry component of the development strategy.[142] At the June 2011 St. Petersburg International Economic Forum, Medvedev endorsed Khloponin's additional proposal to attract foreign direct investment of some 300 billion rubles on the basis of a 60 billion rubles initial investment to lay down infrastructure in the first 4 years followed by 240 billion rubles in tax breaks and investment.[143]

Credit Suisse and the United Arab Republic's (UAR) Abu Dhabi Investment Company (Invest AD) have already declared their readiness to invest in the project. Included among these plans is the KBR's 2008 plan for five major investment projects that would be able to entertain 25,000 visitors at any one time and provide 20,000 jobs. In 2009 the South Korean company Hanok and Russia's Olimp agreed to invest 600 million euros in Elbrus to build 300 kilometers of trails, eight lifts totaling 100 kilometers, a skating rink, hotel, and sports complexes.[144] Following a joint statement on development of the North Caucasus by President Medvedev and French leader Nicolas Sarkozy during the G8 summit in Deauville, France's *Caisse des Depots et Consignations* holding company signed an investment agreement at the June 2011 St. Petersburg Economic Forum.[145]

Local Policy.

Each Muslim republic where the CE has a permanent network—Chechnya, Dagestan, Ingushetia, and the KBR—has its own style and counterinsurgency and counterterrorism (anti-jihadism) policies. Under Ramzan Kadyrov's brutal rule, Chechnya maintains the harshest regime, while Ingushetia and the KBR have taken a softer line with the arrival of new presidents, and Dagestan falls in the middle between Ramzan Kadyrov's harsh rule and the more conciliatory line in Ingushetia and the KBR. Kadyrov has made some gains in reducing insurgent and terrorist activity in Chechnya, which by 2010 was the least active of the CE's four main vilaiyats in terms of the number of jihadi attacks and related casualties. This result has been achieved through a mixture of the carrot and the stick, with a clear emphasis on the latter but with far less violence than that inflicted by the mujahedin. Localized counterterrorist operations are carried out ruthlessly, on occasion with casualties among civilians or innocent family members of mujahedin. Abductions, though fewer and sometimes driven by blood revenge rather than jihad-related problems, continue at a somewhat lower level in several of the Caucasus republics. Kadyrov's policy towards the families of mujahedin differs significantly from that of his North Caucasus counterparts. The families of known or suspected mujahedin are often harassed, detained, and beaten, and their homes are occasionally demolished. Such policies negate any progress Kadyrov has made in the battle for "hearts and minds" by attempting to co-opt the banner of Islam claimed by the CE. This co-optation effort has been built around the construction of Europe's largest mosque and an Islamic university and moderately enforcing some Islamic holidays and customs, including restrictions on female dress. At the same time, Kadyrov, like his Caucasus counterparts, has supported the traditional Sufi clerics under theo-ideological and physical attack from the takfirist mujahedin, and he has tried to enlist clerics in efforts to counter the CE's increasingly sophisticated and effective propaganda.

Ingushetia President Yunusbek Yevkurov has employed a very different policy — the most liberal policy of any North Caucasus leader — initiating a sea change from Zyazikov's brutal regime and showing enormous courage in the process. Upon assuming office in 2008, he reached out to the nationalist and democratic opposition, offering them positions in his government, and created an advisory body of societal and opposition organizations. Yevkurov also moved aggressively to talk young Muslims out of joining the jihad and into leaving it, working with families, councils of village elders, and *teip* or clan councils.[146] According to Yevkurov, 16 mujahedin were convinced to turn themselves in during 2009 and 36 in 2010, and there were only 15 mujahedin active in the republic by early 2010.[147] In some cases, the courts applied no punishment to those who surrendered, and many were provided work or education.[148]

Yevkurov was targeted by Buryatskii in a car bomb assassination attempt in June 2009 that left the Ingush President severely wounded. Nevertheless, after rehabilitation, Yevkurov returned to work within 2 months, publicly forgave his attackers, and continued to work with families of mujahedin to convince them to leave the jihad. In February 2010, Yevkurov reiterated the cornerstone of his anti-jihadism policy of "showing good will towards those who have deviated from the law" and even offered mujahedin an amnesty of sorts, promising that if mujahedin turned themselves in, they would receive soft sentences and would be eased back into society:

> Today a unique opportunity has been created, and a chance to become a fully engaged citizen of society included in the process of the economic rebirth of our Ingushetia, applying your strength and knowledge in creative places of work and showing yourselves favorably in any of the spheres of social and public political life, is still being preserved for each of you [mujahedin].[149]

Two days after Buryatskii's demise in March 2010, Yevkurov met with the relatives of those who had sheltered Buryatskii and the other mujahedin who were planning a major terrorist attack in Ingushetia.

Yevkurov told these families and, by extension, all Ingushetia's families, that they should know who is coming into their homes. He added that the authorities would continue his policy of trying to persuade mujahedin to abandon jihad, but that the security infrastructure would go into action for those who could not be persuaded.[150] Similarly, Yevkurov has led in reducing violent outcomes of the notoriously violent Caucasus tradition of blood feuds that contribute to both jihadi and non-jihadi violence in the region. In a 2-year period, the Ingush authorities reconciled 150 families, according to Yevkurov, in part by raising the ransom for resolving them from 100 thousand rubles to one million rubles.[151]

Compared to his colleagues in the North Caucasus, which is plagued more by corruption than any other region, Yevkurov has carried out the most aggressive anti-corruption campaign. Greater social expenditures and economic investment plus Yevkurov's struggle against corruption and clean bookkeeping is improving the situation, but slowly. Yevkurov policies have allowed Ingushetia to double its revenues from 810 million rubles in 2008 to 1.744 billion rubles in 2010![152] This is not to say that Yevkurov has ignored the stick. In early January, rumors claimed that Yevkurov had requested 20 units of additional military intelligence (GRU) forces for the republic.[153] However, whereas Kadyrov has overemphasized the "stick" of hard power, Yevkurov has heavily favored the "carrot" of soft power. Yevkurov's policies have corresponded with a significant decline in the number of attacks in Ingushetia, according to my own estimates, from some 138 in 2008 and 175 in 2009, to only 99 in 2010 and approximately 40 in the first 6 months of 2011.[154] However, it remains unclear whether Yevkurov's policies are responsible for the decline, factoring in the killing of Buryatskii and the capture of CE military amir and GV amir "Magas" Ali Taziyev.

Since Putin's removal of the ailing Valerii Kokov (the KBR's ancient Soviet-era communist party first secretary) from the KBR presidency in 2005, the republic has adopted policies closer to Yevkurov's. Like Zyazikov, Kokov had been harshly criticized by official Islamic clergy, the general populace, young Muslim Islamists, and jihadists. He was replaced by the energetic 48-year-old ethnic Kabardin businessman Arsen Kanokov. He immediately moved to address the concerns of Muslims as well as the ethnic Balkar minority. Kanokov replaced the republic's premier with an ethnic Balkar and its hard-line MVD chief Khachim Shogenov with an ethnic Russian, Yurii Tomchak. Shogenov had been sharply criticized by almost everyone in the republic, including the KBR's DUM, for his heavy-handed and broad-brushed crackdown on Muslims in 2003-04 in an effort to contain the burgeoning jihadi movement in the republic. Tomchak took immediate steps to assuage the KBR's Muslims, especially the more volatile young generation, including the inclusion of KBR DUM representatives on the MVD's public council. The ministry also signed a cooperation agreement with the DUM and other confessions' public organizations.[155] Not a single jihadi attack was carried out in the KBR in 2006.[156] KBR DUM chairman, mufti Anas Pshikhachev, quickly acknowledged the MVD's efforts under Tomchak to address the DUM's grievances but warned that the threat of Islamic extremism persists in the KBR.[157] In addition, Kanokov set aside 4.5 million rubles in April 2007 for the construction of two new mosques in the capital Nalchik. The closing of mosques by the authorities in

2004 had helped spark the rise of the jihadist combat jamaat "Yarmuk" in 2004 and irritated moderate Muslims and official clergy alike. Kanokov also attracted new investments for developing tourism in the Elbrus District resort area.

However, rather than seeing a decline in jihadi attacks, Kanokov presided over a marked increase: 28 in 2008, 23 in 2009, and 113 in 2010, despite amir Astemirov's demise in March 2010.[158] In January 2011, OVKBK mujahedin killed chief mufti of the KBR's DUM, Anas Pshikhachev, in the republic's capital of Nalchik. The KBR plunged into a state of desperation. In February, the Council of Elders of the Balkar people called for the introduction of direct federal rule and Kanokov's resignation. Kanokov, speaking before the KBR parliament, appealed to the federal authorities for additional assistance in combating jihadism in the republic, adding that the mujahedin "are not afraid."[159] At the end of February, the OVKBK carried out the noted series of attacks across the Elbrus resort area. In May, the OVKBK attempted to assassinate Kanokov in the largest attack in the KBR since Basaev's and Astemirov's October 2005 Nalchik raid by exploding a bomb under the VIP reviewing stand at a horse racing track during Nalchik's May Day festivities. The attack killed at least one civilian, a 97-year-old Great Patriotic War veteran, and wounded some 40 civilians and officials. Among the wounded were the KBR's Culture Minister Ruslan Firov and former MVD chief Khachim Shogenov.[160] At this point, Kanokov or someone in the KBR may have adopted Kadyrov's approach of forming special units to fight the mujahedin. A group calling itself the "Black Hawks" (chernyie yastreby) declared war on the OVKBK, but nothing much seems to have come of the group. In

April, security forces killed Astemirov's successor, OVKBK amir "Abdullah" Asker Dzhappuev, along with his naibs and several other top OVKBK amirs. Since then, there has been a slight decline in the rate of attacks in the KBR.

In Dagestan, today the CE's spearhead, a new president and his team, have borrowed more elements from Yevkurov than from Kadyrov. Unlike Chechnya, the origins of jihadism in Dagestan are driven entirely by intra-confessional tensions created by the emergence of a significant Salafi community at odds with traditional Sufis. Successive leaders have failed to resolve the religious tensions. In February 2006, Putin replaced long-standing ethnic Dargin Dagestan President Magomedali Magomedov with the ethnic Avar chairman of Dagestan's Legislative Assembly, Mukhu Aliev. His tenure saw a steady increase in jihadi activity and no perceptible improvement in the civility of counterinsurgency and counterterrorism polices in the region. Aliev was replaced in 2010 with Magomedov's son, Magomedsalem Magomedov, who endeavored to engage the Salafi community in Dagestan, coordinating the formation of a council of Salafi Islamic scholars (ulema), which drafted a series of demands for the government to meet. According to the Russian human rights group "Memorial," a government representative was authorized to meet with the council, but the dialogue has not produced notable results other than the regular appearance of Salafi representatives at public ceremonies. Magomedov has also endeavored to replicate Yevkurov's efforts in Ingushetia by succeeding in enticing some young mujahedin from the forest and back to civilian life, and institutionalizing the process in November 2010 in the form of an adaptation commission. The commission includes the imam of Dagestan's Central Mosque and the head of the Salafist umbrella organization, Akhlyu-s-sunna, A. K. Kebedov and is chaired by Rizvan Kurbanov, deputy premier in charge of the power ministries in the republic who personally led talks with prospective defectors from the mujahedin. Kurbanov was described by Memorial as "open to representatives of civil society, reacted without fail, personally, and immediately to reports about the crudest violations of human rights . . . met with the relatives of abductees, [and] cooperated with lawyers in specific cases."[161] Magomedov has also worked on the economy. Dagestan's government has developed a joint project with the majority state-owned Russian Copper Company to develop the North Caucasus's largest ore deposit of Kizil-Dere in southern Dagestan's Ahtynsky District. The mining project plus the accompanying development of transport infrastructure and utilities should provide considerable employment.[162] Another investment project for the region is Dagestani oligarch Suleiman Kerimov's purchase of the republic's Anzhi Makhachkala (AM) premier soccer team. This is being followed up by further investments of $1.4 billion by Kermiov into AM's stadium and Makhachkala hotels and AM's recent $30 million purchase of global soccer superstar Samuel Eto'o in August 2011. Kerimov is also investing in the North Caucasus tourist resort cluster project.[163]

During his still short tenure, Magomedov's new course has yielded few results unless one can show that jihadi violence would be even more prevalent without his policies. The CE's DV has been able to step up its violence, threatening Magomedov and killing numerous government officials. Since April 2010, the DV has been the most prolific of the CE's vilaiyats in

57

terms of number of attacks, including suicide bombings, with approximately 267 total attacks (including
six suicide attacks) in 2010 and 200 attacks (including three suicide attacks) during the first 6 months of
2011, compared to 144 total attacks, including one suicide bombing, in 2009.[164] Nor is there a demonstrable
improvement in the republic's human rights record,
either.[165]

Siloviki.

A key problem is that neither the republic presidents nor SKFO envoy Khloponin exercise much, if
any, control over the siloviki as the latter continue to
violate Muslim citizens' human, civil, and political
rights. How much Moscow or the civilian leadership
controls federal forces in the North Caucasus also remains a question, though not their responsibility for
rights violations. Both federal forces and local police,
often working jointly in counter-terrorist operations,
continue to employ detention on the basis of mere
suspicion and falsified evidence, beatings, and torture
during detentions, and extrajudicial punishments, including abductions and killings. The European Court
for Human Rights continues to hand down judgments
against Russian authorities regarding such violations.[166]

Federal forces still deployed in the region include
military, FSB specially designated forces (spetsnaz),
and GRU. MVD forces, which according to federal law
are supposed to be under federal control, are often
an object of contestation in numerous regions across
Russia. Kadyrov appears to control not only his own
forces but the MVD and perhaps its Internal Troops in
Chechnya, both of which have made incursions into

Ingushetia sometimes coordinated with Ingushetia's MVD and sometimes not. Military forces, including new mountain fighting forces created a few years ago and based in Botlikh (Dagestan) and Zelenchukskaya (Karachaevo-Cherkessia), maintain a low profile, remaining on their bases. In rare cases when military units are called upon to take part in counterterrorist operations, military helicopters, and more rarely artillery are called in to target mujahedin uncovered in mountainous areas. For example, CE amir Umarov's naib Supyan Abduallev was killed in March 2011 in an operation that used helicopters and artillery. Military and other convoys occasionally come under ambush by mujahedin in all four of the main republics where the CE maintains a permanent presence. The creation of the National Anti-Terrorism Committee (NAK) and regional counterparts appears to have improved coordination and intelligence-sharing between the various power ministries. Security and police forces have become proficient in tracking and killing leading amirs, but they have been less successful in capturing high value targets that would provide invaluable additional intelligence. The only such case was the July 2010 capture of GV amir and CE military amir "Magas" Ali Taziyev; ever since, the Ingushetia mujahedin's fortunes have been in steady decline.

Chechnya's Kadyrov maintains considerable control over MVD forces in his republic and deploys his own presidential guards, which in the past have come into conflict with special battalions subordinated to federal power ministries and led by the leaders of families and teips or clans in competition with Kadyrov as a counterweight to Kadyrov's power. In 2010 the federal authorities decided that the dire situation in Dagestan required a new approach. It was decided to replicate the Chechenization of the conflict in Chechnya under Kadyrov with the formation of special battalions under the control of various federal organs of coercion, and by establishing under the Dagestan MVD a separate volunteer special motorized battalion of native Dagestanis for carrying out counterinsurgency operations. The first 300 volunteers were trained by November 2010, with another 400 intended to complete the 700-man force.[167] There is no evidence that this measure has produced any appreciable results.

In sum, Russian and North Caucasus authorities' continuing rights violations largely, if not entirely, negate the positive development of an increased use of soft power methods in fighting jihadism pushed by Medvedev, Yevkurov, and Kanokov. However counterintuitive it may be, the steepest decline in jihadi activity has occurred in the republics with the harshest policy line, Kadyrov's Chechnya, and the softest, Yevkurov's Ingushetia.

THEORETICAL AND POLICY IMPLICATIONS

The rise of the CE, and attendant theoretical concepts, have concrete security policy implications for Russia, the United States, and globally. The CE's rise refutes many widespread assumptions, biases, hypotheses, and theories extant in the scholarly, analytical, activist, and policymaking communities regarding the violence in the North Caucasus and the organization and causality of terrorism and jihadism in general. The CE's continuing capability to recruit and attack is not simply a response to Russian brutality and poor governance, but is also a consequence of the CE's effective deployment of jihadi propaganda, training, leadership, and substantial ties to AQ, as well as the global jihadi revolutionary alliance, and an umma in the throes of radicalism and revolution. The CE's long-standing though evolving relationship with AQ and the larger global movement and its organization and structure do not confirm the leaderless jihad hypothesis which argues that AQ has lost much of its relevance and the global jihadi movement is devolving into a diffusion of atomized lone wolves.[168] Similarly, the CE's own decentralized network structure and functioning and the nature of its relationship with AQ and the global jihadi alliance supports a more traditional view of a network inspired and loosely grouped around AQ and its affiliates. The CE, like the inspirational, if not institutional, AQ hub and more nodal elements among the global jihad's innumerable groups, is likewise decentralized, but it retains a hub consisting of Umarov and top amirs and qadis and loosely coordinating interconnected nodes or vilaiyats working largely independently but towards one and the same set of goals: The creation of an Islamist CE state and a confederated global caliphate.

If one regards AQ as the inspirational core, if not the organizational leader, of a highly decentralized global jihadi revolutionary movement, then a conceptualization of the CE's place would find it several degrees removed from the core, comprised of AQ central and affiliates like AQAP and AQ in the Maghreb (AQIM). Groups like the Taliban and Lashkar-e-Toiba comprise the first concentric circle around the AQ core because of both their involvement in international attacks and their deep involvement with, and geographical proximity to AQ central. The CE's position is similar to that of as-Shabaab in Somali and other groups in the second concentric circle, since they are not located near and do not cooperate as closely with

AQ central, are only just beginning to participate in international operations, and prefer to, or because of resource shortages must, focus largely on establishing their local emirate. The third concentric circle would be lone wolves inspired by but having no ties to a formal jihadi group. The fourth, most outer concentric circle lies outside the alliance but within the movement. It consists of groups that ascribe to the violent establishment of their own Islamist government but reject the goal of creating a caliphate and cooperation with other global jihadi revolutionary groups.

Nor do patterns in the CE correlate with the conclusion put forward by Robert Pape that suicide terrorism is largely a response to foreign occupation, having little or no connection to jihadi ideology or goals.[169] Leaving aside the fact that suicide terrorism is almost exclusively a jihadist phenomenon, this mono-causal explanation is simplistic, especially when it comes to any jihadi organization, including the North Caucasus. CE suicide bombers' videotaped martyrdom testaments state explicitly that their motivation is to "raise the banner of Allah above all others." The CE's chief propagandist and organizer of suicide terrorism from mid-2008 to early 2010, Sheikh Said Abu Saad Buryatskii was an ethnic Buryat-Russian, converted to Islam, and never set foot in the Caucasus until spring 2008 after he returned from abroad to study Islam in Egypt and Kuwait. The goals and strategy of the CE and other global jihadi revolutionary groups are not simply local or defensive, seeking merely to drive out occupiers, but are explicitly offensive and expansionist. Thus, the CE's expansionist goals aimed at seizing all of Russia and the Transcaucasus and recreating the Islamist caliphate defuse Pape's theory.

These theoretical conclusions have policy implications: First, the CE's ties to AQ, its own sophisticated organization and decentralized functioning, and its religious rather than nationalist motives are transforming it from a local to an international actor and emerging threat. Second, even if it were, like the ChRI, only a threat to Russian national security, this threat would still have international security implications, since Russia remains an important Eurasian power and is emerging as a useful ally of the United States and the West in the war against jihadism. Third, the CE's emergence as a transnational threat with growing radicalization, capacity, and aspirations marks a newly emerging threat to U.S. national and international security. Fourth, the CE's transformation and integration into the global jihadi revolutionary alliance demonstrate the ability of AQ and its affiliated movements to evolve, adapt, and flourish in response to Western counter-jihadism efforts. Fifth, the global jihadi revolutionary alliance's ability to evolve and adapt is facilitated by the existence of the larger jihadi and Islamist social movements emerging from a pre-revolutionary Muslim world that includes democratic, nationalist, communist, Islamist, and jihadist forces. Sixth, except in the most failed states like Yemen and Somalia, the groups that make up the global jihadi revolutionary alliance are unlikely to seize power precisely because of the limited appeal of their narrow and strict ideological orientation. Seventh, given this larger revolutionary and radicalizing context, international, Western, Eurasian, American, and Russian security are likely to be threatened by this revolution's intended and unintended destabilizing and violent effects for decades to come; the most virulent of which are the global jihadi revolutionary alliance and its individual groups. Finally, the jihadi revolutionary alliance's globalism dictates a global and cooperative response on the part of those whom it targets.

Operationally, Caucasus jihadists are now recruits for major terrorist attacks against the West. Sheikh al-Maqdisi has designated the CE as the global jihad's bridgehead into Eastern Europe, as evidenced by the CE inserted cells into Belgium and the Czech Republic and its apparent involvement in its first international terrorist plot in Belgium. The CE itself could attempt to attack U.S. targets in Russia or elsewhere, including the northern supply route for U.S. and NATO troops fighting in Afghanistan. Its most capacious DV and its Azerbaijan Jamaat put Umarov within striking range of international and U.S. interests in Azerbaijan such as oil company headquarters, refineries, and the Baku-Tbilisi-Ceyhan pipeline carrying oil to Europe. Clearly, a CE or other significant jihadi presence in Azerbaijan would have security implications for the entire Transcaucasus and the Persian Gulf region. In addition, the CE is a recruiting ground of mujahedin for other fronts in the global jihad. Moreover, Russia has the largest stockpiles of chemical, biological, radiological, and nuclear materials and WMD in the world. The CE adds potential demand to this supply. In the past, there have been reports of Chechen separatist and Caucasus jihadi attempts to acquire WMD in Russia, and the CE websites' posting of the famous 2003 Al-Fahd fatwa three times in 2010 suggests that some in the CE may wish to obtain them.

Given the emerging CE threat, the U.S. Government should maximize cooperation across Eurasia to include Russia, the Collective Security Treaty Organization (CSTO), and the Shanghai Cooperation Organization (SCO) in the war against jihadism. The United

States and Europe should also attempt to stabilize the Caucasus by resolving the Azeri-Armenian conflict over Nagorno-Karabakh and at least minimizing Russian-Georgian tensions, so these do not play into the hands of CE or other jihadists. One goal might be to rein in Georgian efforts to whip up trouble in the North Caucasus, especially among the Muslim Circassian ethnic groups. Tbilisi has opened up a television and radio company that broadcasts anti-Russian propaganda to the region, and some Georgian opposition figures and one former U.S. official have claimed that President Mikheil Saakashvili's government is providing financial and training assistance to the CE.[170] Speculating on the Circassian genocide issue as the Sochi Olympics approach, Tbilisi adopted a parliamentary resolution calling for a boycott of the Sochi games and for Russian and international recognition of the Tsarist forces' rout and exile of the Circassians in the 1860s as a genocide. Georgia's policies could radicalize some Circassians and thus improve the CE prospects for recruitment and attacking the Sochi games. Tbilisi also waived visa requirements for Iranians and North Caucasus residents, which could facilitate the movement of global jihadists from South Asia and the Persian Gulf region to the North Caucasus and Europe.

Finally, Western-Eurasian (NATO-CSTO) cooperation can be used to nudge Eurasia's authoritarian regimes, including Moscow, to conduct their anti-jihadism and other policies with a greater eye towards citizens' human, civil and political rights, and the implications of all of the above for the war against jihadism. Only with broad and effective regional cooperation involving all of the post-Soviet states will the United States and the West be able to defeat the global jihadi threat.

ENDNOTES - CHAPTER 1

1. Interview with Basaev in Oleg Blotskii, "Terroristy proni-kayut v Rossiyu za dengi," *Nezavisimaya gazeta*, March 12, 1996, cited in James Hughes, *Chechnya: From Nationalism to Jihad*, Philadelphia, PA: University of Pennsylvania Press, 2007, pp. 101, 154.

2. Gordon M. Hahn, *Russia's Islamic Threat*, New Haven, CT, and London, UK: Yale University Press, 2007.

3. "Aslan Maskhadov: 'My sozdadim polnotsennoe Islams-koe Gosudarstvo," *Kavkaz tsentr*, March 8, 2010, 15:55, available from *www.kavkazcenter.com/russ/content/2010/03/08/71101.shtml*; "Abdallakh Shamil Abu-Idris: 'My oderzhali strategicheskuyu pobedu,'" *Kavkaz-Tsentr*, January 9, 2006, 08:47:10, available from *www.kavkazcenter.net/russ/content/2006/01/09/40869.shtml*; "Prezident ChRI Sheik Abdul-Khalim. Kto On?" *Kavkaz-Tsentr*, March 12, 2005, 00:59:07, available from *www.kavkazcenter.com/russ/content/2005/03/12/31285.shtml*; Aleksandr Ignatenko, "Vakhkhab-itskoe kvazigosudarstvo," *Russkii Zhurnal*, available from *www.russ.ru/publish/96073701*, citing the Chechen militants' website, *Kavkaz-Tsentr*, September 10, 2002; Paul Murphy, *The Wolves of Islam: Russia and the Faces of Chechen Terrorism*, Dulles, VA: Brassey's Inc., 2004, pp. 171-75; and Hahn, *Russia's Islamic Threat*, pp. 40-64.

4. Available from *www.islamdin.com/index.php?option=com_con tent&view=category&id=4&Itemid=28*. The audios are available from *www.islamdin.com/index.php?option=com_content&view=category &id=33&Itemid=31*. The videos are available from *www.islamdin. com/index.php?option=com_content&view=category&id=7&Itemid=8*.

5. For example, see "Usama bin Laden ob' yasnaet khadis Kaba bin Malika," *Kavkaz tsentr*, April 12, 2011, 01:08, available from *www.kavkazcenter.com/russ/content/2011/04/12/80669. shtml*; "AL'-kaida: Sheikh Usama bin Laden obratilsya k frant-suzskomu narodu," *Kavkaz tsentr*, January 21, 2011, 21:44, available from *www.kavkazcenter.com/russ/content/2011/01/21/78402. shtml*; "Sheikh Aiman az-Zavakhiri: 'Dagestan—osvozhde-nie posle otchayaniya'," *Umma News*, January 20, 2011, 00:07, available from *ummanews.com/minbar/359-----l----r.html*; "Pri-soediniyaites' k Karavanu," *Islamdin.com*, February 19, 2009, 12:09, available from *www.islamdin.com/index.php?option=com_*

content&view=article&id=278:2009-02-19-12-11-52&catid=4:2009-02-04-14-07-09&Itemid=28; Ibrakhim Abu Ubeidulakh, "Zashchita Usamy Bin Ladena ot napadok murdzhiitov, nechestivtsev!," *Islamdin.com*, January 4, 2010, available from *www.islamdin.com/ index.php?option=com_content&view=article&id=609:2010-01-04-23-52-10&catid=8:2009-02-04-22-51-14&Itemid=26*; "Sheikh Usama Bin Laden-Imam Mudzhakhidov Nashei Epokhi," *Jamaat Shariat*, January 7, 2010, 12:53, available from *www.jamaatshariat.com/ru/ content/view/414/29/*; *Hunafa.com*'s video compilation "Oh, He Who Rebrukes Me," bin Laden and the CE's Sheikh Said Abu Saad Buryatskii, "O, uprekayushchii menya," available from *Hunafa.com*.

6. Some of the other jihadi sheiks, scholars, and propagandists prominent on CE websites include: medieval source of jihadi thought Taki al-Din Ahmad Ibn Taimiyya; the Egyptian scholar and Muslim Brotherhood leading figure, Sayyid Qutb; the Pakistani Salafist and jihadi revolutionary, Sayed Abul Ala Maududi; the London-based Syrian sheikh, Sheikh Abu Basyr At-Tartusi; Sheikh and Imam, Abdullah bin Abdu-Rakhman bin Jibrin; Ibrahim Muhammad Al-Hukail; Iraqi Sheikh and mujahed, Addullah Ibn Muhammad Ar-Rashud; Sheikh Muhammad Salih al-Munajid; and Sheikh Abdurrakhman Al-Barrak.

7. "Zhurnal 'Vdokhnovlai': 'Sdelai bombu v Maminoi kukhne'," *Islamdin.com*, December 3, 2010, available from *www.islamdin. com/index.php?option=com_content&view=article&id=992:2010-12-03-10-29-08&catid=43:2010-11-25-17-50-11&Itemid=33*; "Zhurnal 'Vdokhnovlyai': Operatsiya 'Krovotechenie'," *Islamdin.com*, December 8, 2010, 11:51, available from *www.islamdin.com/index. php?option=com_content&view=article&id=999:2010-12-08-11-56-36&catid=27:2009-02-09-17-38-17&Itemid=16*; "V internete rasprostranen vtoroi nomer zhurnala 'Al-Kaidy', *Inspire*, Vdokhnovenie, *Kavkaz tsentr*, October 12, 2010, 12:07, available from *www. kavkazcenter.com/russ/content/2010/10/12/75767.shtml*; and Gordon M. Hahn, *Islam, Islamism, and Politics in Eurasia Report*, International Institute of Professional Education and Research (IIPER), No. 40, May 2011, available from *www.miis.edu/media/view/23115/ original/kavkazjihad_montrep_iiper_40_may_2011.pdf*.

8. "Executive Report," *Militant Ideology Atlas*, West Point, NY: U.S. Military Academy, Combating Terrorism Center, November 2006, pp. 7-8.

9. "Amir Saifullakh o knige sheikha Abu Mukhammada al' Makdisi 'Milleti Ibrakhim'," *Islamdin.com*, February 18, 2010, 08:03, available from *www.islamdin.com/index.php?option=com_ content&view=article&id=656:-q-q-&catid=7:2009-02-04-15-45- 20&Itemid=8*; and "Amir Saifullakh: 'O Tavkhide'—1 chast'," *Islamdin.com*, February 15, 2010, 01:37:27, available from *www. islamdin.com/index.php?option=com_content&view=article&id=651:- q-q-1-&catid=7:2009-02-04-15-45-20&Itemid=8*.

10. See, for example, "A message from Sheikh al-Maqdisi to the Mujahedeen of the Caucasus Emirate," *Kavkaz tsentr*, September 18, 2009, 16:55, available from *www.kavkazcenter.com/eng/ content/2009/09/18/11018.shtml*, first published in Arabic on al-Maqdisi's site *Almaqdese.net*, 15 Ramadan 1430, available from *almaqdese.net/r?i=07090901*. See also "Nastavlenie mudzhakhi-dam ot sheikh Abu Mukhammada al' Makdisi," *Islamdin.com*, March 13, 2011, 23:37, available from *www.islamdin.com/index. php?option=com_content&view=article&id=1077:2011-03-14-00-00- 13&catid=4:2009-02-04-14-07-09&Itemid=28*; "Pis'mo ot Sheikha Abu Mukhammad Al-Makdisi," *Kavkaz tsentr*, February 5, 2011, 13:50, available from *www.kavkazcenter.com/russ/content /2011/02/05/78885.shtml*; and "Razmyshleniya, imam Abu Muk-hammad Al'-Makdisi," *Hunafa.com*, December 11, 2009, 12:00, available from *hunafa.com/?p=2530*.

11. "A message from Sheikh al-Maqdisi to the Mujahedeen of the Caucasus Emirate," *Kavkaz tsentr*, September 18, 2009, 16:55, available from *www.kavkazcenter.com/eng/content/2009/09/18/11018. shtml*; first published in Arabic on al-Maqdisi's site, *Almaqdese.net*, 15 Ramadan 1430, available from *almaqdese.net/r?i=07090901*.

12. "Fatva Sheikha Abu Mukhammada al'-Makdisi, da ykrepit ego Allakh," *Kavkaz tsentr*, September 10, 2010, 20:55, available from *www.kavkazcenter.com/russ/content/2010/09/10/75149.shtml*.

13. "Amir Seifullah o protsesse podgotovki k provoglash-eniyu Kavkazskogo Emirata," *Kavkaz tsentr*, November 20, 2007, 23:15, available from *www.kavkazcenter.com/russ/content/2007/ 11/20/54479.shtml*.

14. On Astemirov's view of the amir's unilateral powers, see "Amir Seifullah o protsesse podgotovki k provoglasheniyu Kavkazskogo Emirata," *Kavkaz tsentr*, November 20, 2007, 23:15, available from *www.kavkazcenter.com/russ/content/2007/11/20/54479.shtml*. For the same by Astemirov's successors, see "Amir Seifullakh Gubdenskii, ra: Ot togo, chto my zdes' voyuem, my nichego ne vyigraem," *JamaatShariat.com*, November 12, 2010, 05:17, available from *www.jamaatshariat.com/-mainmenu-29/14-facty/1345-2010-11-12-02-18-12.html*; and "Kadii IK Ali Abu MukhIammad o pravlenii, dzhikhade, o polozhenii shakhidov i mnogom drugom," *Guraba.info*, June 28, 2011, 10:57, available from *www.guraba.info/2011-02-27-17-59-21/30-video/1107--i-.html*.

15. CE qadi Astemirov passed down a death sentence against London exile and former ChRI foreign minister Akhmed Zakaev when he broke with the CE upon its creation in October 2007. See "Shariatskii sud vynes reshenie po dely Zakaeva," *Kavkaz tsentr*, August 25, 2009, 02:45, available from *www.kavkazcenter.com/russ/content/2009/08/25/67586.shtml* and *www.islamdin.com/index.php?option=com_content&view=article&id=467:2009-08-24-21-30-20&catid=10:2009-02-06-21-56-11&Itemid=26*. The CE's Dagestan Vilaiyat (DV) qadis have even passed down, and the DV mujahedin have consequently carried out, two known death sentences against Dagestani citizens. In July 2010, then DV qadi and soon-to-be CE qadi Abu Muhamad al-Dagistani issued a death sentence against Salimhan Shagidkhanov, condemned for adultery and raping a Muslim woman. Al-Dagistani issued a second death fatwa against Patimat Magomedova, a female headmaster accused of kicking school girls out of class for wearing the *hijab*. After each of the accused was executed, the verdicts were posted on *JamaatShariat.com* as a warning to those who would dare noncompliance with Shariah. "V Vilaiyate Dagestan progovoren Shariatskom sudom i unichtozhen vrag Allakha Shagidkhanov Salimkhan," *JamaatShariat.com*, August 10, 2010, 13:56, available from *www.jamaatshariat.com/new/15-new/1095-2010-08-10-10-58-30.html*; and "Zayavlenie Spetsial'noi operativnoi gruppy mudzhakhidov dagestanskogo fronta: Prigovor priveden v ispolnenie," *Jamaat Shariat.com*, September 25, 2010, 15:24, available from *www.jamaatshariat.com/new/15-new/1298-2010-09-25-12-47-36.html*.

16. "Otvety na voprosy k"adiya Imarata Kavkaz, amira Ob"edinennogo Vilaiyata Kabardy, Balkarii i Karachya, Saiful-

lakha," *Islamdin.com*, December 12, 2010, 14:54, available from *www.islamdin.com/index.php?option=com_content&view=article &id=594:2009-12-12-14-58-15&catid=27:2009-02-09-17-38-17&Itemid=16.*

17. "Amir Saifullakh o knige sheikha Abu Mukhammada al' Makdisi 'Milleti Ibrakhim'," and "Otvety na voprosy k'adiya Imarata Kavkaz, amira Ob'edinennogo Vilaiyata Kabardy, Balkarii i Karachaya, Saifullakha."

18. See, for example, the writings of Said Abu Saad Buryatskii, Aleksandr Tikhomirov, the CE's leading propagandist and operative for suicide bombings in 2008 and 2009, especially: Said Abu Saad Buryatskii, "Vzglyad na Dzhikhad iznutri: Geroi Istiny i Izhi," *Hunafa.info*, May 30, 2009, 1:01, available from *hunafa.com??p=1534*; and Said Abu Saad Buryatskii, "Vzglyad na Dzhikhad iznutri: Geroi istiny i Izhi, Chast' 2," *Hunafa.info*, June 24, 2009, 4:04, available from *hunafa.info/?p=1715*. See also the final istishkhad testament of his student, "Zaveshchanie Abdul-Malika: 'Ya ukhozhu na Istishkhad, chtoby pozhertvovat' svoei dushoi vo imya Allakha!'," *Kavkaz tsentr*, July 29, 2010, 12:04, available from *www.kavkazcenter.com/russ/content/2010/07/29/74167.shtml.*

19. In 2002, the ChRI's jihadist wing had convinced Maskhadov of the need to jihadize the ChRI's constitution and expand their operations across the North Caucasus and Russia. "Amir Imarata Kavkaz Doku Abu Usman: 'Mudzhakhidy Provozglasili Imarat Kavkaz i ya gorzhus' etim," *KavkazInform.com*, May 27, 2010, 05:13, available from *www.kavkazinform.com/2011-05-27-02-00-06/3-2011-05-27-05-14-31.html*. The first result was the October 2002 Dubrovka Theatre hostage taking. According to a CE biography of the late Dagestan amir and CE Shariah Court "qadi" (chief magistrate) Magomedali Vagabov, a.k.a. Seifullah Gubdenskii, in autumn 2003 Vagabov and his fellow mujahedin wanted to go to Chechnya and to fight but were ordered to remain near Khasavyurt, Dagestan, "in connection with a decision of Maskhadov and Basaev *to spread combat to the entire territory of the Caucasus*" (my italics), "Amir Dagestanskogo Fronta i K"adii Imarata Kavkaz Saifullakh. Chast' 2—Dzhikhad," *Jamaat Shariat. com*, August 13, 2010, 02:50, available from *jamaatshariat.com/ru/-mainmenu-29/14-facty/1105--2-.html*. For the interview of Ichkeria Republic President Aslan Maskhadov and Chairman of the Shar-

iat Committee of Ichkeria Republic's State Defense Committee Abdul-Khalim, Sadulaev, see "'My perenosim voinu na territoriyu vraga. . . .'," *Kavkaz-Tsentr*, August 1, 2004, 13:09:21, available from *www.kavkazcenter.com/russ/content/2004/08/01/24101.shtml*. In an August 1, 2004, interview Maskhadov portrayed himself as a devout Muslim but purely nationalist freedom fighter, but he also publicly supported the creation of a broad Muslim cohort of insurgents for actions throughout the North Caucasus, and indeed all of Russia. Seated next to his designated successor and ChRI Shariah Court Chairman Abdul-Khalim Sadulaev for a joint interview, Maskhadov warned: "We are capable of carrying out such operations in Ichkeria, Ingushetiya and Russia, and we will prove it." See "'My perenosim voinu na territoriyu vraga. . .'," *Kavkaz-Tsentr*, August 1, 2004, 13:09:21, available from *www.kavkazcenter. com/russ/content/2004/08/01/24101.shtml*. After Maskhadov's death in March 2005, new ChRI president Sadulaev created the North Caucasus and Dagestan Fronts in May 2005, demonstrating his intent to spread the jihad across the North Caucasus. The North Caucasus Front included Ingushetia and Kabardino-Balkaria Sectors. See "ukazom Prezidenta ChRI Sadulaeva sozdan Kavkazskii front," *Kavkaz tsentr*, May 16, 2005, 00:54:35, available from *www. kavkazcenter.com/russ/content/2005/05/16/33965.shtml*. Upon his succession of Sadulaev in June 2006, Umarov created the Volga and Urals Fronts in order to target Tatarstan, Bashkortostan, and other Russian Federation regions with significant Muslim Tatar and Bashkir populations. See "Prezident ChRI podpisal ukazy o sozdanii Uralskogo i Povolzhskgo frontov," *Kavkaz-Tsentr*, July 9, 2007, 14:34, available from *www.kavkazcenter.com/russ/ content/2006/07/09/45779.shtml*. In January 2006, Basaev, encouraged by Kabardin mujahedin like Anzor Astemirov and Musa Mukozhev, convinced ChRI president Sadulaev to create a council of ulema, Islamic scholars, in preparation for the declaration of the Caucasus Emirate (CE), but Sadulaev and Basaev were killed in June and July, respectively, leaving the task to Umarov. "Amir Imarata Kavkaz Doku Abu Usman: 'Mudzhakhidy Provozglasili Imarat Kavkaz i ya gorzhus' etim."

20. For the full declaration, see "Ofitsial'nyi reliz zayavleniya Amira Dokki Umarova o provozglashenii Kavkazskogo Emirata," *Kavkaz tsentr*, November 21, 2007, available from *www. kavkazcenter.com/russ/content/2007/11/21/54480.shtml*; and "Komu vygodna provokatsiay pod nazvaniem 'Kavkazskii Emirat',"

Chechenpress.org, October 29, 2007, available from *www.chechen-press.org/events/2007/10/29/04.shtml*.

21. "Amir Dokku Abu Usman o bin Ladene, Imarate Ka-vkaz I poteryakh modzhakhedov," Kavkaz tsentr, May 17, 2011, 00:01, available from *www.kavkazcenter.com/russ/content/2011/05/17/81607.shtml*. The English translation is available from *www.kavkazcenter.com/eng/content/2011/05/17/14313.shtml*.

22. See, for example, Testimony of Miriam Lanskoy, "Hu-man Rights in the North Caucasus," Tom Lantos Human Rights Commission, U.S. Congress, April 15, 2011, available from *tlhrc. house.gov/docs/transcripts/2011_04_15_North_Caucasus/Lanskoy_Testimony.pdf*; "Miriam Lanskaya o terakte v Domodedovo i mo-mente istiny," *Caucasus Times*, February 2, 2011, available from *www.caucasustimes.com/article.asp?id=20748*; Robert Pape, Lindsey O'Rourke, and Jenna McDermit, "What Makes Chechen Women So Dangerous?" *New York Times*, March 31, 2010; and Mairbek Vatchagaev, "Arrests in Europe Place 100,000 Member Chechen Diaspora in the Spotlight," Jamestown Foundation *Eurasia Daily Monitor*, Vol. 7, Issue 215, December 2, 2010, 01:13, available from *www.jamestown.org/single/?no_cache=1&tx_ttnews%5Btt_news%5D=37230&tx_ttnews%5BbackPid%5D=7&cHash=85a84a8365*.

23. "Ofitsial'nyi reliz zayavleniya Amira Dokki Umarova o provozglashenii Kavkazskogo Emirata," and "Obrashchenie amira IK Dokku Abu Usman k musulmanam Egipta i Tunis," *Ja-maatShariat.com*, available from *www.jamaatshariat.com*.

24. "Raz'yasnenie Amira IK Dokku Abu Usman v svy-azi s fitnoi sredi modzhakhedov," *Kavkaz tsentr*, October 18, 2010, 12:51, available from *www.kavkazcenter.com/russ/content /2010/10/18/75902.shtml*.

25. Abu-t-Tanvir Kavkazskii, "Vchera, segodnya, zavtra . . . ," *Hunafa.com*, April 24, 2010, 11:23, available from *hunafa. com/?p=3451*.

26. "Stennogramma video: Kadii IK Abu Mukhammad—'Otvety na voprosy'—1 chast'," *Guraba.info*, July 8, 2011, 00:18, available from *guraba.info/2011-02-27-17-59-21/30-video/1117--i-q-q-1-.html*; and VDagestan.info, July 8, 2011, available from

vdagestan.info/2011/07/08/%d0%ba%d0%b0%d0%b4%d0%b 8%d0%b9-%d0%b8%d0%ba-%d0%b0%d0%b1%d1%83-%d0 %bc%d1%83%d1%85i%d0%b0%d0%bc%d0%bc%d0%b0%d 0%b4-%d0%be%d1%82%d0%b2%d0%b5%d1%82%d1%8b- %d0%bd%d0%b0-%d0%b2%d0%be%d0%bf%d1%80%d0%be/.

27. The CE's DV mujahedin provided a somewhat explicit description of this strategy in "Perekhvat initsiativy," *Jamaat Shariat,* June 2, 2010, 03:29, available from *www.jamaatshariat.com/ru/- mainmenu-29/14--/834-2010-06-02-03-05-02.html.*

28. "Amir Imarata Kavkaz Dokku Abu Usman: 'My osvo- bodim Krasnodarskii krai, Astrakhan i Povolzhskii zemli . . .'", *Kavkaz tsentr,* March 8, 2010, 11:38, available from *www.kavkazcenter. com/russ/content/2010/03/08/71087.shtml.*

29. These include, according to my own estimate, some 30 in the last 2 months of 2007, 373 in 2008, 511 in 2009, 583 in 2010, and some 300 in the first 5 months of 2011.

30. Gordon M. Hahn, "The Caucasus Emirate's 'Year of the Offensive' in Figures: Data and Analysis of the Caucasus Emir- ate's Terrorist Activity in 2009," *Islam, Islamism, and Politics in Eur- asia Report* (henceforth *IIPER*), No. 7, January 18, 2010; Gordon M. Hahn, "Comparing the Level of Caucasus Emirate Terrorist Activ- ity in 2008 and 2009," *IIPER,* No. 8, February 5, 2010; Gordon M. Hahn, "Trends in Jihadist Violence in Russia During 2010 in Statis- tics," *IIPER,* No. 33, January 26, 2011; and Gordon M. Hahn, "CE- Affiliated Website Reports Number of Jihadi Attacks and Result- ing Casualties from January Through June 2011," *IIPER,* No. 44, August 12, 2011, all available from *www.miis.edu/academics/faculty /ghahn/report.*

31. "Fatalities by Year and Month as Part of Operation 'En- during Freedom' in All Theatres of Operation," *Icasulaties.org,* available from *icasualties.org/oef/ByMonth.aspx;* "Operation En- during Freedom: U.S. Wounded Totals," *Icasualties.org,* available from *icasualties.org/OEF/USCasualtiesByState.aspx.*

32. See the video "Majlis al-Shura of the Caucasus Emirate – 25 April 2009," *You Tube, www.youtube.com/watch?v=DQQKPNfmo1U.* For the English translation of Umarov's post-Shura declaration

with a link to his downloadable video statement in Russian, see "Amir Dokka Abu Usman: 'This Year Will Be Our Offensive Year'," *Kavkaz tsentr*, May 17, 2009, 15:17, available from *www.kavkaz.tv/eng/content/2009/05/17/10700.shtml*.

33. See, for example, Said Abu Saad, Buryatskii, "Istishkhad mezhdu pravdoi i lozh'yu," *Hunafa.com*, December 9, 2009, 1:01, available from *hunafa.com/?p=2514*; "Said abu Saad. Ob rezultatakh operatsii v Nazrani 17 avgusta 2009g," *Hunafa.com*, September 7, 2009, 11:23, available from *hunafa.com/?p=1984*; Said Abu Saad Buryatskii, "Vzglyad na Dzhikhad iznutri: Geroi Istiny i lzhi," *Hunafa.info*, May 30, 2009, 1:01, available from *hunafa.com??p=1534*; Said Abu Saad Buryatskii, "Vzglyad na Dzhikhad iznutri: Geroi istiny i lzhi, Chast' 2," *Hunafa.info*, June 24, 2009, 4:04, available from *hunafa.info/?p=1715*; and "Said Abu Saad. Vzglyad na Dzhikhad iznutri: Geroi Istiny i lzhi, Chast' 3," *Hunafa.com*, July 24, 2009, 1:01, available from *hunafa.com??p=1855*.

34. Umarov appeared in a videotape released shortly after the bombing along with the Riyadus Salikhiin Martyrs Brigade's (RSMB) amir Khamzat and the suicide bomber, Magomed Yevloev, before the latter was dispatched to Moscow. See "Video: Amir Imarata Kavkaz Dokku Abu Usman posetil bazu Brigady Shakhidov Riyadus Salikhin i sdelal zayavlenie," *Kavkaz tsentr*, February 4, 2011, 23:18, available from *www.kavkazcenter.com/russ/content/2011/02/04/78877.shtml*; and "Obrashchenie amira Imarata Kavkaz Dokku Abu Usman v svyazi s Shakhidskoi operatsiei v Moskve 24 yanvarya 2011 goda" at "Amir Dokku Abu Usman: 'Spetsoperatsiya v Moskve byla provedena po moemu prikazu'," *Kavkaz tsentr*, February 7, 2011, 22:58, available from *www.kavkazcenter.com/russ/content/2011/02/07/78967.shtml*.

35. Then U.S. State Department Deputy Chief for C.I.S. Affairs Stephen Sestanovich told the Senate Foreign Relations Committee in his November 1999 testimony: "Chechen insurgents are receiving help from radical groups in other countries, including Osama bin Laden's network and others who have attacked or threatened Americans and American interests." See "Text: Sestanovich Statement on Chechnya to Senate Committee, November 4," *GlobalSecurity.com*, USIS Washington File, November 4, 1999; and *www.globalsecurity.org/military/library/news/1999/11/991104-chechen-usia1.htm*. See also then U.S. National Security Council

adviser Richard Clarke's comments regarding ChRI-AQ ties on the Charlie Rose Show, PBS, November 30, 1999, available from *www.charlierose.com/view/interview/3968*; and then U.S. Congressional Task Force on Terrorism and Unconventional Warfare Director Joseph Bodansky's comments on ChRI-AQ ties in Joseph Bodansky, "Chechnya: The Mujahedin Factor," *Freeman.org*, 1999, available from *www.freeman.org/m_online/bodansky/chechnya.htm*.

36. Defense Intelligence Agency Declassified *Swift Knight Report*, Document No. 3095345, no date, *Judicial Watch*, available from *www.judicialwatch.org/cases/102/dia.pdf*.

37. *Ibid.*, p. 4.

38. *Ibid.*

39. *Ibid.*, pp. 3-4.

40. *Ibid.*, p. 5.

41. On Al-Haramain, see "Al-Haramain Islamic Foundation v. United States Department of the Treasury, Hearing No. 10-350," Ninth Circuit Court, March 9, 2011, available from *www.ca9. uscourts.gov/media/view_subpage.php?pk_id=0000007126*; and the U.S. government's sentencing memorandum, evidentiary exhibits, and a Russian FSB officer's testimony about al-Haramian's assistance to Chechen and Dagestani mujahedin in "United States of America v. Perouz Sedaghaty, Case No. 05-CR-60008-HO," United States District Court for the State of Oregon, November 23, 2010, available from the Investigative Project, *www. investigativeproject.org/documents/case_docs/1422.pdf#page=65*.

42. See Federal Bureau of Investigation Special Agent Robert Walker's "Affidavit in Support of Complaint Benevolence International Foundation, Inc. and Emman M. Arnout, a.k.a. Abu Mahmood, a.k.a. Abdel Samia," April 29, 2002, in the 2002 case, "The United States of America v. Benevolence International Foundation, Inc. and Emman M. Arnout," *Investigative Project*, p. 3, available from *www.investigativeproject.org/documents/case_docs/94. pdf* (henceforth Walker Affadavit).

43. "Treasury Designates Benevolence International Foundation and Related Entities as Financiers of Terrorism," Press Release, U.S. Department of Treasury's Office of Public Affairs, PO-3632, November 19, 2002, available from *www.investigativeproject. org/documents/case_docs/1176.pdf.*

44. Walker Affidavit, p. 3.

45. Walker Affidavit, pp. 3, 24-28.

46. One disc of videos was viewed by the author and deposited by him in the archives at the Hoover Institution, Stanford University.

47. "Indictment in United States of America v. Babar Ahmad, aka Babar Ahmed, and Azzam Publications," *Investigative Project*, no date, pp. 1, 5-9, and 12-13, available from *www.investigative project.org/documents/case_docs/96.pdf.*

48. Walker Affidavit, pp. 24-28.

49. Rohan Gunaratna, *Inside Al Qaeda: Global Network of Terror*, New York: Columbia University Press, 2002, p. 180; and S. Pryganov, *Vtorzhenie v Rossiyu*, Moscow, Russia: Eksprint, 2003, pp. 189-90.

50. "Chechen commander Basayev vows more attacks," BBC Monitoring, in Johnson's Russia List, November 2, 2004, citing *Kavkaz tsentr*; see also *The Globe and Mail*, November 2, 2004, available from *www.theglobeandmail.com/servlet/ArticleNews/TPStory/ LAC/20041102/CHECHEN02/TPInternational/?query=basayev.*

51. "Militants Target Arabs in Massive Fundraising Campaign for Chechen Insurgents," *Transnational Security Issues Report*, December 13, 2007; and "Amir Seifullakh Gubdenskii, (ra): Ot togo, chto my zdes' voyuem, my nichego ne vyigraem," *JamaatShariat. com*, November 12, 2010, 05:17, available from *www.jamaatshariat. com/-mainmenu-29/14-facty/1345-2010-11-12-02-18-12.html.*

52. Swift Knight Report, p. 3.

53. *Ibid.*, p. 5.

54. Gunaratna, *Inside Al Qaeda*, p. 179.

55. RFERL Newsline, Vol. 7, No. 60, March 28, 2003; RFERL Russian Federation Report, Vol. 4, No. 14, April 17, 2002; "Russia's 'Taliban' Faces Uneasy Future after Guantanamo Torment," *AFP*, August 1, 2004; and *Regions.ru*, March 27, 2003, available from *www.regions.ru*.

56. The account does not make it precisely clear whether Vagabov himself went to Afghanistan. "Amir Dagestanskogo Fronta i K adii Imarata Kavkaz Saifullakh. Chast' 2—Dzhikhad." *Jamaat Shariat*, August 13, 2010, 02:50, available from *jamaatshariat.com/ru/-mainmenu-29/14-facty/1105--2-.html*.

57. "Czech Police Arrest Suspected Russia's North Caucasus Terrorists," *BNO News*, May 3, 2011, 2:27, available from *wireupdate.com/wires/17128/czech-police-arrest-suspected-russias-north-caucasus-terrorists/*.

58. The Bulgar Jamaat's Russian-language website is available from *tawba.info* or *jamaatbulgar.narod.ru*. For the call for jihad against Russia, see "Obrashchenie Dzhamaata Bulgar k Musul'manam Rossii, Jammat Bulgar," February 28, 2009, available from *jamaatbulgar.narod.ru/statiy/v1_28-02-09.htm*. See also Laith Alkhouri, "'Jamaat Bulgar' Website—'About Us' Section—Provides Background Information on Ties to Taliban, Tactics," *Flashpoint Intel*, April 29, 2010, available from *www.flashpoint-intel.com/images/documents/pdf/0410/flashpoint_jamaatbulgaraboutus.pdf*.

59. Brian Glynn Williams, "Shattering the Al-Qaeda-Chechen Myth," Jamestown Foundation *Chechen Weekly*, Vol. 4, No. 40, November 6, 2003; Brian Glyn Williams, "Allah's Foot Soldiers: An Assessment of the Role of Foreign Fighters and Al-Qa-ida in the Chechen Insurgency," in Moshe Gammer, ed., *Ethno-Nationalism, Islam and the State in the Caucasus: Post-Soviet Disorder*, London, UK: Routledge, 2007, pp. 156-78; and Brian Glynn Williams, Keynote Lecture, International Conference, "The Northern Caucasus: Russia's Tinderbox," Washington, DC: Center for Strategic and International Studies, November 30-December 1, 2010.

60. This is according to Iraqi Interior Minister Falah al-Naqib. See "Iraq's Al-Naqib—'Terrorists' From Chechnya, Sudan, and Syria Killed Arrested," *Beirut LBC SAT Television*, 1300 GMT, January 30, 2005.

61. See Gunaratna, *Inside Al Qaeda*, p. 292.

62. The four were 18-year-old Sergey Viktorovich Vysotskiy, 20-year-old Timur Vladimirovich Khozkov, 20-year-old Aslan Yerikovich Imkodzhayev, and a 20-year-old Dagestani national who calls himself Abu Abdul. "Vlasti Livana obvinyayut v terrorizme chetyrekh grazhdan Rossii," *Kavkaz uzel*, October 5, 2007, available from *www.kavkaz.memo.ru/newstext/news/id/1198805.html*; and "Four Russian Citizens Accused of Terrorism in Lebanon," *Retwa.org*, October 5, 2007, available from *www.retwa.org/home.cfm?articleId=4834*, citing *Kavkaz uzel*, available from *www.kavkaz-uzel.ru*.

63. Luiza Orazaeva, "NAK: ubityi v Kabardino-Balkarii boevik obuchalsya v Livane," *Kavkaz-uzel.ru*, March 16, 2011, 21:45, available from *www.kavkaz-uzel.ru/articles/182411/*.

64. Dagestani mujahed Yasin Rasulov has written convincingly about this in Yasin Rasulov, *Dzhikhad na Severnom Kavkaze: storonniki i protivniki, Kavkaz tsentr*, pp. 18-29 and 55-59, available from *www.kavkazcenter.com/russ/islam/jihad_in_ncaucasus/PDF_version.pdf*. Rasulov was killed by Russian forces in 2007; he uses reliable pre-communist Russian Muslim scholarly sources to document his claims.

65. The extent to which the Russian conquest and the Caucasus, especially Dagestani resistance in the 19th century, were marked by an intra-Caucasus struggle between *gazavatists*, defending local sovereignty and the customs of *adat* and Sufism, and pro-Shariah quasi-Islamists like Imam Shamil, Gazi Mukhammad, and Kuraly-Magoma, sometimes backed by the Iranian Shah, is often overlooked. See, for example, N. I. Pokrovskii, *Kavkazskie Voiny i Imamat Shamilya*, Moscow, Russia: ROSSPEN, 2009.

66. Rasulov, *Dzhikhad na Severnom Kavkaze: storonniki i protivniki*.

67. Olga Bobrova, "Imarat Kavkaz: Gosudarstvo kotoro-go net," *Novaya gazeta*, No. 27, March 17, 2010, available from *www.novayagazeta.ru/data/2010/027/18.html*; and Oleg Guseinov, "Stroite'stvo khrama Marii Magdaliny priostanovlena iz-za otsu-tsviya sredstv," *Gazeta yuga*, April 21, 2005, available from *www.gazetayuga.ru/archive/2005/16.htm*.

68. Aleksandr Zhukov, *Kabardino-Balkariya: Na puti k katastofe*, Legal Defense Center 'Memorial', *Kavkaz uzel*, Appendix 9, avail-able from *www.kavkaz-uzel.ru/analyticstext/analytics/id/1231255. html*; Hahn, *Russia's Islamic Threat*, pp. 152-65; "Amir Seifullah o protsesse podgotovki k provoglasheniyu Kavkazskogo Emirata"; Gordon M. Hahn, "Profile of 'Seifullah' Anzor Astemirov, Part 3: Astemirov and the Caucasus Emirate," *IIPER*, No. 23, September 13, 2010, available from *www.miis.edu/media/view/21434/original/ kavkazjihad_montrep_iiper_23_sept_2010.pdf*; "Amir Seifullah: 'Po-beda ot Allakha, tak zhe kak i porazhenie'," *Kavkaz-Tsentr*, May 29, 2006, 03:34, and May 30, 2006, 04:34, available from *www. kavkazcenter.net/russ/content/2006/05/29/44895*; Aleksandr Zhukov, "Religioznyi raskol i politicheskoe reshenie," *Polit.ru*, May 18, 2006, 08:25, available from *www.polit.ru/analytics/2006/05/18/ kanokov.html*.

69. "Amir Seifullah o protsesse podgotovki k provoglash-eniyu Kavkazskogo Emirata"; Hahn, "Profile of 'Seifullah' Anzor Astemirov, Part 3: Astemirov and the Caucasus Emirate"; and "Shamil sprosil menya: 'Kogda stanesh' Amirom, ty ob' yavish' Imarat?'," *Kavkaz tsentr*, August 30, 2011, 02:19, available from *www.kavkazcenter.com/russ/content/2011/08/30/84755.shtml*.

70. "Aleksandr Tikhomirov, Sheikh Said Abu Sadd al-Bury-atii-Said Buryatskii," *Kavkaz uzel*, August 17, 2009, 17:02, avail-able from *www.kavkaz-uzel.ru/articles/158565*; and "Kadyrov naz-val Saida Buryatskogo 'ideologom terakta, nakachivayushchim smertnikov tabletkami," July 30, 2009, 11:39, available from *www. kavkazcenter.com/russ/content/2009/07/30/67080.shtml*; and Said Abu Saad Buryatskii, "Vzglyad na Dzhikhad iznutri: Geroi Istiny i lzhi," *Hunafa.info*, May 30, 2009, 1:01, available from *hunafa. com??p=1534*.

71. *Ibid.* One source reports that Buryatskii supposedly visited the North Caucasus as early as the late 1990s and at that time declared his loyalty to the mujahedin before he traveled to Egypt and other countries in the Middle East to receive a "Wahhabist" education. Alena Larina, "Poslednii spektakl'," *Rossiiskaya gazeta*, March 5, 2010, available from *www.rg.ru/2010/03/05/said-bur-site.html*. Buryatskii's conversion and radicalization might have been connected to his relationship with Bakhtiyar Umarov, no relation to the CE's amir, a local imam in Ulan-Ude formerly from Uzbekistan. In November 2008, Bakhtiyar Umarov was arrested in Russia, charged with having ties to the radical international Islamist party, 'Hizb ut-Tahrir Islami', and had his recently granted Russian passport confiscated. The CE-affiliated site *Kavkaz tsentr* claimed locals were sure imam Umarov's arrest was a consequence of his association with Buryatskii. "Buryatiya. Arestovan znakomyi Sheikha Saida Burtaskogo imam Bakhtiyar Umarov," *Kavkaz tsentr*, November 21, 2008, 07:53, available from *www.kavkazcenter.com/russ/content/2008/11/21/62314.shtml*.

72. Said Abu Saad Buryatskii, "Vzglyad na Dzhikhad iznutri: Geroi istiny i lzhi, Chast' 2," *Hunafa.info*, June 24, 2009, 4:04, available from *hunafa.info/?p=1715*.

73. "Aleksandr Tikhomirov, Sheikh Said Abu Sadd al-Buryatii—Said Buryatskii."

74. Buryatskii, "Vzglyad na Dzhikhad iznutri: Geroi istiny i lzhi, Chast' 2"; Video "How I went to Jihad and What I have seen here (English subtitles)—Sheikh Sayeed of Buratia 1," *'i24 sishan tschetschenien jihad islam nasheed qoqaz kaukasus'*, *You Tube*, June 17, 2009, *www.youtube.com/watch?v=XgE19xcasEg*; Said Abu Saad, Buryatskii, "Said Buryatskii: 'Vzglyad na dzhikhad isnutri, po proshestvii goda," *Imam TV*, May 18, 2009, *http://imamtv.com/news-18-05-1009.htm* citing *Hunafa.com*; and "Aleksandr Tikhomirov, Sheikh Said Abu Saad al-Buryatii—Said Buryatskii."

75. Hahn, "The Caucasus Emirate's 'Year of the Offensive' in Figures: Data and Analysis of the Caucasus Emirate's Terrorist Activity in 2009"; and Hahn, "Comparing the Level of Caucasus Emirate Terrorist Activity in 2008 and 2009."

76. On these ethnic Slav CE operatives and their terrorist attacks and plots, see Gordon M. Hahn, "Alleged Russian Jihadi Suicide Bomber Viktor Dvorakovskii Captured," *IIPER*, No. 43, July 21, 2011, available from *www.miis.edu/media/view/21196/original/KAVKAZJIHAD_MonTREP_IIPER_20_Aug2010.pdf*; Gordon M. Hahn, "Kosolapov Re-emerges Ahead of Peak Jihadi Fighting Season," *IIPER*, No. 41, May 27, 2011, available from *www.miis.edu/media/view/23146/original/kavkazjihad_montrep_iiper_41_june_2011.pdf*; and Gordon M. Hahn, "Two More Suicide Bombings," *IIPER*, No. 35, February 18, 2011, available from *www.miis.edu/media/view/22492/original/kavkazjihad_montrep_iiper_35_feb_2011.pdf*.

77. "Amir Dagestanskogo Fronta i K'adii Imarata Kavkaz Saifullakh. Chast' 1—Do Dzhikhada," *Jamaat Shariat*, August 8, 2010, 21:58, available from *jamaatshariat.com/ru/fakty/29-facty/1089-2010-08-08-21-40-39.html*.

78. "Amir Dagestanskogo Fronta i K'adii Imarata Kavkaz Saifullakh. Chast' 2—Dzhikhad," *Jamaat Shariat*, August 13, 2010, 02:50, available from *jamaatshariat.com/ru/-mainmenu-29/14-facty/1105--2-.html*.

79. Leading jihadism expert Evan Kohlmann describes Ansar as "self-selecting form of internet-based terrorism," "promoting the mission of al-Qa`ida" and "loyal" to AQ. Evan Kohlmann, "A Beacon for Extremists: The Ansar al-Mujahideen Web Forum," *CTC Sentinel*, Vol. 3, Issue 2, February 2010, pp. 1-4, available from *www.ctc.usma.edu/posts/a-beacon-for-extremists-the-ansar-al-mujahideen-web-forum*.

80. "Hammer Time: Ansar al-Mujahideen Webmaster Arrested!," *Jawa Report*, August 31, 2010, available from *mypetjawa.mu.nu/archives/203766.php*.

81. "Fairfax County Man Accused of Providing Material Support to Terrorists," U.S. Attorney General's Office, July 21, 2010, available from *www.justice.gov/usao/vae/Pressreleases/07-JulyPDFArchive/10/20100721chessernr.html*; and "Hammer Time: Ansar al-Mujahideen Webmaster Arrested!"

82. "Hammer Time: Ansar al-Mujahideen Webmaster Arrested!"

83. Kohlmann, "A Beacon for Extremists: The Ansar al-Mujahideen Web Forum."

84. "Announcing the Start of a New Campaign in Support of the Caucasus Emirate," *Alqimmah.net*, December 5, 2010, available from *www.alqimmah.net/showthread.php?t=21139&goto=nextoldest*.

85. "V global'noi seti interneta otkrylsya novyi forum v podderzhku Dzhikhada," *Islamdin*, July 20, 2010, 16:18, available from *www.islamdin.com/index.php?option=com_content&view=article&id=849:2010-07-20-16-49-47&catid=32:2009-03-05-23-19-06&Itemid=29*.

86. According to the Spanish Civil Guard, Errai registered and paid for the hosting of the site for purposes of spreading jihadi propaganda and indoctrinating and recruiting sympathizers to radical Islamism and jihad. "Another Online Jihadi Arrested in Spain," *Jawa Report*, August 31, 2010, available from *mypetjawa.mu.nu/archives/203757.php*.

87. Awlaki proposes creation of fee-free and uncensored discussion fora, lists of e-mail addresses so Muslims interested in jihad can contact each other and exchange information, online publications and distribution of literature and news of the jihad, and sites which focus on separate aspects of the jihad. He urges Muslims to follow the events of the jihad because it "enlivens our connection to the jihad"; "strengthens our belongingness to the Umma"; "approves our joining the jihad"; "inflames our desire to receive martyrdom"; allows Muslims "to see how Allah defends his slaves and leads them to victory"; provides "practical examples on how our brothers are applying theory in contemporary conditions"; and "strengthens our attention to the Koran," to which strengthened ties "[reach their] peak when we ourselves participate in this conflict, jihad, entering the ranks of the mujahedin." "V global'noi seti interneta otkrylsya novyi forum v podderzhku Dzhikhada," *Islamdin.com*, July 20, 2010, 16:18, available from *www.islamdin.com/index.php?option=com_content&view=article&id=849:2010-07-20-16-49-47&catid=32:2009-03-05-23-19-06&Itemid=29*.

88. "Imam Anuar al' Aulyaki: Al-Dzhanna—Chast 1," *Islamdin.com*, July 25, 2010, 06:09, available from *www. islamdin.com/index.php?option=com_content&view=article&id=854:- q-q-1&catid=4:2009-02-04-14-07-09&Itemid=28*; and Anwar Al-Aw-laki, "Akhira: Sudnyi den i Ognennyi ad," *Islamdin.com*, March 25, 22:45, available from *www.islamdin.com/index.php?option=com_ content&view=article&id=1084:2011-03-25-22-51-31&catid=4:2009- 02-04-14-07-09&Itemid=28*

89. Abdallakh Shamil Abu-Idris, "My odrerzhali strate-gicheskyu pobedu," *Kavkaz-Tsentr*, January 9, 2006, 08:47:10, available from *www.kavkazcenter.net/russ/content/2006/01/09/40869. shtml*.

90. "Prezident ChRI podpisal ukazy o sozdanii Uralskogo i Povolzhskgo frontov," *Kavkaz-Tsentr*, July 9, 2007, 14:34, available from *www.kavkazcenter.com/russ/content/2006/07/09/45779.shtml*.

91. A group of Tatar "garage jihadists," the so-called "Islamic Jamaat," was allegedly formed in Tatarstan by ethnic Tatars be-fore it was uncovered and its members tried, convicted, and sen-tenced to various prison sentences in 2008. However, there was no evidence of ties to the CE. Irina Borogan, "Dzhamaat v dva khoda," *Novaya gazeta*, No. 9, February 7, 2008, p. 10, available from *www.novayagazeta.ru/data/09/10.html*.

92. Marat Gareev and El'vira Mirgaziyanova, "Krupnyie ter-akty gotovilis' i v Bashkirii," *Komsomolskaya Pravda*, March 29, 2010, available from *www.kp.ru/daily/24463.5/624739/*.

93. "V Bashkirii 'shyut' delo 'Uiguro-Bulgarskogo dzhamaa-ta,'" *Islam.ru*, April 29, 2009, available from *www.islam.ru/rus/2009- 04-29/*. Dorokhov was killed when he allegedly offered resistance during a search of his residence. His colleague, Rustem Zainagut-dinov was sentenced to 15 years for planning to blow up a barrier separating a water supply tank and an ammonia tank, attack a traffic police post and seize weapons, and seize the Salavat city's FSB building. Stanislav Shakhov and Ivan Panfilov, "KP: V Bash-kirii obezvrezhen terroristicheskii Uiguro-Bulgarskii dzhamaat," *TsentrAzii*, March 29, 2010, 09:30, available from *www.centrasia.ru/ newsA.php?st=1269840600*.

94. In March 2010, after a group of armed men attacked a food store in Oktyabrskii District, Bashkortostan, wounding two seriously, the Bashkortostan Ministry of Internal Affairs (MVD) mounted an operation, eventually capturing a group of 10 Bashkir and two Ingush mujahedin said to be providing funds to the CE and led by one Bashir Allautdinovich Pliev (born 1966) from Ingushetia. "V Bashkirii zaderzhany 8 chlenov religiozno-ekstremistckogo bandpodpol'ya," *Regnum.ru*, March 29, 2010, 10:27, available from *www.regnum.ru/news/1267599.html*; and "Uderzhan esho odin uchastnik ekstrimistskogo bandpodpol'ya," *Regnum.ru*, April 1, 2010, 19:04, available from *www.regnum.ru/news/fd-volga/bash/1269348.html*. In July another jihadi jamaat was allegedly involved in a series of attacks on police and planning some 18 more, including on gas pipelines, in Bashkortostan, and perm Oblast. "Obstrelyavshikh post DPS ishchet polk militsii," *Lifenews.ru*, July 4, 2010, 16:55, and July 5, 2010, 20:06, *lifenews.ru/news/30293*, 08:25, available from *www.kavkazcenter.com/russ/content/2010/07/05/73590.shtml*; "V Bashkortostane atakovan blokpost okkupatsionnoi bandy DPS," *Kavkaz tsentr*, July 5, 2010, 00:20; "Viktor Palagin: 'Ekstremistov vovse ne shef FSB pridumal," *MediaKorSet*, December 16, 2011, 21:43, available from *www.mkset.ru/news/person/13353/*; and Tatyana Maiorov, "V Bashkirr minuvshim letom predotvratili neskol'ko teraktov," *Rossiiskaya gazeta*, December 17, 2010, available from *www.rg.ru/2010/12/17/reg-bashkortostan/fsb-anons.html*. In February 2011, another group of four mujahedin was uncovered in the Oktyabrskii District of Bashkiriya. Its members were charged with illegal weapons possession and illegal production of and intent to use explosives. They were said to have "extremist literature," and the official arrest report stated that one of the arrestees was the amir of the "Oktyabrskii Jamaat" and that the jamaat was part of the CE. "Alleged Islamic Extremists Detained In Russia's Bashkortostan," *RFERL*, February 8, 2011, available from *www.rferl.org/content/bashkortostan_islamists/2301430.html*. In Tatarstan, a jihadist cell allegedly tied to *Hizb ut-Tahrir Islami* was uncovered and destroyed in November 2010. "Likvidirovannnyie v Tatarstane terroristy byli islamistami," *Regnum.ru*, November 25, 2010, 14:48, available from *www.regnum.ru/news/fd-volga/tatarstan/1350137.html*. A series of incidents involving alleged mujahedin occurred in Astrakhan in late 2010 and early 2011. See Gordon M.

Hahn, "More Evidence of Jihadism in Astrakhan," *IIPER*, No. 41, May 27, 2011, available from *www.miis.edu/media/view/23146/ original/kavkazjihad_montrep_iiper_41_june_2011.pdf*; and Gordon M. Hahn, "Is There an Astrakhan Jamaat?," *IIPER*, No. 36, March 11, 2011, available from *www.miis.edu/media/view/22714/original/ kavkazjihad_montrep_iiper_36_mar_2011.pdf*.

95. "Zayavlenie o granitsakh vilaiyat Idel-Ural," *Kavkaz tsentr*, January 26, 2011, 21:12, available from *www.kavkazcenter.com/russ/ content/2011/01/26/78553.shtml*; and "Pis'mo v redaktsiyu: Ob-rashchenie modzhakhedov Idel-Ural k modzhakhedam Imarata Kavkaz," *Kavkaz tsentr*, February 1, 2011, 00:03, available from *www.kavkazcenter.com/russ/content/2011/02/01/78726.shtml*.

96. The failed 2010 New Year's Eve Moscow plot involved several Stavropol residents, who, in turn, were friends or acquaintances with several ethnic Russian mujahedin who converted to Islam, including the abovementioned ethnic Russian, Islamic-convert couple, Vitalii Razdobudko and Marina Khorosheva, who carried out separate suicide bombings in Gubden, Dagestan, on February 14, 2011, and Viktor Dvorakovskii, who was wanted for 5 months and finally captured in July 2011.

97. Video "Shura amirov Dagestana. Bayat Amira Dagestana Khasana, October 19, 2010," *JamaatShariat.com*, December 1, 2010, available from *www.jamaatshariat.com/ru*; and *Kavkaz tsentr*, December 1, 2010, available from *www.kavkazcenter.com*.

98. "Press-Sluzhba Amira DF: My gordy uchasti nashikh brat'ev, nashi ubityie—v Rayu, vashi—c Adu," *Jamaat Shariat*, August 22, 2010, 17:53, available from *jamaatshariat.com/-main-menu-29/14-facty/1152-2010-08-22-17-00-31.html*.

99. Sochi and the southern Krasnodar are native lands of ethnic Circassian Adygs; the Kabards, and Cherkess of the Republic of Kabardino-Balkaria (KBR) and Karachaevo-Cherkessiya (KChR) respectively, are also Circassian ethnic groups. The locus for much of the Olympic Games is located on Red Hill, known as the spot of the last battle of the Circassians against the Russians, which ended in their defeat and eventual deportation and exile of many Circassians abroad.

100. The attacks included a truck bomb targeting a resort hotel that was uncovered and disarmed and the bombing of support pillars for a ski lift that brought down over 40 of its cabins and necessitated closure of the resort for several days. See Gordon M. Hahn, "The OVKBK's Sochi Vector," *IIPER*, No. 36, March 11, 2011, available from *www.miis.edu/media/view/22714/original/ kavkazjihad_montrep_iiper_36_mar_2011.pdf*.

101. CE maps depict the future emirate's territory as comprising the entire North Caucasus, including predominantly ethnic-Russian populated regions like the abovementioned Krasnodar and Stavropol Territories. But both Russian territory north of the CE's North Caucasus and the Transcaucasus south of the North Caucasus—that is, Georgia, Armenia, and Azerbaijan—are labeled "occupied Muslim lands." See "Ideyu otdeleniya Kavkaz est smysli obsuzhdat,' chtoby lishit' islamistov znameni borby . . .!," *Kavkaz tsentr*, February 12, 2011, 11:15, available from *www. kavkazcenter.com/russ/content/2011/02/12/79121.shtml*; and "Posol SShA v Moskve o neizbezhnom ob"edinenie musul'man Severnogo Kavkaza," *Kavkaz tsentr*, December 6, 2010, 09:18, available from *www.kavkazcenter.com/russ/content/2010/12/06/77052.shtml*.

102. Likely CE mujahedin from Dagestan have been crossing Azerbaijan's border recently, engaging battle in the north with Baku's army and police. A recent indigenous jihadist attack on Baku's Shiite-led Juma mosque underscores the point. An armed Wahhabi group led by a former Azeri army officer Kyamran Asadov was uncovered in October 2007 plotting to attack state institutions and blow up U.S. and other Western embassies in Azerbaijan. In 2008, a jihadist group previously active in Chechnya and Dagestan was uncovered in Baku by Azeri intelligence.

103. Video, "Shura amirov Dagestana," Bayat Amira Dagestana Khasana, October 19, 2010."

104. Rose revolution leaders and former Saakashvili allies, such as the former parliament speaker Nino Burjanadze and former Defense Minister Irakly Okruashvili, have claimed that Tbilisi has been training Ingush mujahedin and that Georgian banks have facilitated money transfers to the Caucasus mujahedin. "Burjanadze Talks About Danger of one more War

from Russia," *Georgian Journal*, October 21, 2010, available from *georgianjournal.ge/index.php?option=com_content&view=article&i d=664:burjanadze-talks-about-danger-of-one-more-war-from-russia- &catid=9:news&Itemid=8*; and "Burjanadze Slams Visa Provocations," *Interfax*, October 21, 2010, 19:01, available from *www. interfax.com/newsinf.asp?pg=2&id=197175*. Former U.S. Foreign Service officer and U.S. Senate Republican Policy Committee foreign policy analyst, James George Jatras claims that in December 2009, a secret meeting took place in Tbilisi with "representatives of numerous jihad groups based in various Islamic and European countries for the purpose of coordinating their activities on Russia's southern flank." According to Jatras, "the meeting was organized under the auspices of high officials of the Georgian government." Although Saakashvili did not attend, Georgian MVD officials and "others acted as hosts and coordinators," and the Georgian ambassador to Kuwait "purportedly facilitated" the participants' travel "from the Middle East." Finally, "[I]n addition to 'military' operations (i.e., attacks in southern Russia) special attention was given to ideological warfare, for example, launching of the Russian-language TV station 'First Caucasus'." James Jatras, "The Georgian Imbroglio—And a Choice for the United States," *America-Russia Net*, February 14, 2010, available from *www.america-russia.net/eng/face/236661338?user_session=4827e878c 0267ddbdd6ee738f8212f1d*.

105. Saoud Mekhennet and Michael Moss, "Europeans Are Being Trained in Pakistani Terrorism Camps, Officials Fear," *New York Times*, September 10, 2007, p. A8.

106. "IJU: Message from the Mujahideen of the Khorasan to the Caucasus Emirate," *Kavkaz Jihad Blogspot*, March 14, 2011, available from *kavkaz-jihad.blogspot.com/2011/03/message-of-mujahideen- from-khorasan-to.html*; and "Video Badr at-Tawheed 'Mensaje de los mujahidines del Jorasán al Emirato del Cáucaso," *Jihad-e-Informacion*, March 2011, available from *jihad-e-informacion.blogspot. com/2011/03/video-badr-at-tawheed-mensaje-de-los.html*.

107. *Ibid.*

108. "Tadzhikistan: Shakhid atakoval bazu RUBOP Sogdiiskii oblasti," *Kavkaz tsentr*, September 3, 2010, 11:39, available from *www.kavkazcenter.com/russ/content/2010/09/03/75000.*

shtml; and "Tadzhikistan: Otvetstvennost' za Shakhidskuyu ataku v Khudzhande vzyala na sebya organizarsiya 'Dzhamaat Ansarullakh'," *Kavkaz tsentr*, September 8, 2010, 12:23, available from *www.kavkazcenter.com/russ/content/2010/09/08/75108.shtml*. On these attacks, see also "MVD Tadzhikistana: Pri vzryve u zdaniya ROBOP v Khudzhande pogib militsioner, smertnikov bylo neskol'ko," *Ferghana.ru*, September 3, 2010, 14:26, available from *www.ferghana.ru/news.php?id=15461&mode=snews*; "Perestrelka s beglymi zaklyuchennymi proizoshlo v Tadzhikistane, rossiiskie voennyie v operatsii ne uchastvuyut," Materik, September 8, 2010, 11:21:16, available from *materik.ru/rubric/detail.php?ID=10653*; "Tadzhikistan: Po faktu vzryva v nochnom klube v Dushanbe zaderzhany dvoe podzrevaemykh," *Ferghana.ru*, September 6, 2010, 10:14, available from *www.ferghana.ru/news.php?id=15470&mode=snews*; and "GKNB Tadzhikistana: Nochnoi vzryv v disko-klube 'Dusti' — khuliganstvo, a ne terakt," *Ferghana.ru*, September 6, 2010, 13:57, available from *www.ferghana.ru/news.php?id=15475&mode=snews*.

109. "Obraschenie Kazakhstanskogo dzhamaata 'Ansaru-d-din'," *Hunafa.com*, November 10, 2010, 1:01, available from *hunafa.com/?p=3839*; and "Vopros o zakonnosti voennikh deistvii v Kazakhstane," *Hunafa.com*, March 18, 2011, 1:01, available from *hunafa.com/?p=4831#more-4831*; and "Vopros o zakonnosti voennikh deistvii v Kazakhstane," *Kavkaz tsentr*, March 19, 2011, 12:16, available from *www.kavkazcenter.com/russ/content/2011/03/19/80081.shtml*.

110. Kazakhstan has played down the terrorist and religious nature of the May 17, 2011 suicide bombing and May 24 car bombing in Alma-Ata or the killing of several policemen on July 7 in Aqtobe. "Vakhkhabity Velikoi Stepi," *Nezavismaya gazeta – Religii*, July 20, 2011, available from *religion.ng.ru/problems/2011-07-20/4_vahhabity.html*; "Kazakhstan Suicide Bombing Puts Spotlight on Western Regions," *Eurasianet.org*, May 24, 2011, 2:10, available from *www.eurasianet.org/node/63549*; "Two die in Kazakhstan car blast," AFP, May 24 2011, available from *news.smh.com.au/breaking-news-world/two-die-in-kazakhstan-car-blast-20110524-1f1zk.html*; "Suicide Bomber has Shahid Belt in Blast in Kazakhstan," *RETWA*, May 17, 2011, available from *www.retwa.com/home.cfm?articleId=11372*; "Kazakh City Hit By Suicide Blast, First Known Attack Of Its Kind," *Radio Free Europe/Radio*

Liberty, May 17, 2011, available from *www.rferl.org/content/kazakh-stan_suicide_bomber/24177028.html*; "Suicide bomber attacks Kazakh secret police HQ ," *Telegraph*, May 17, 2011, available from *www.telegraph.co.uk/news/worldnews/asia/kazakhstan/8518895/Suicide-bomber-attacks-Kazakh-secret-police-HQ.html*; and "Blast Kills Two Outside Kazakh Security Service Building," *Radio Free Europe/Radio Liberty*, May 24, 2011 09:02, available from *www.rferl.org/content/blast_outside_security_service_building_kazakh_capital/24184422.html*.

111. "Modzhahedi Kyrgyzstana prisyagnuli Amiry Islamskogo Emirata Afghanistan Myllo Omary," *Kavkaz tsentr*, March 22, 2011, 12:51, availale from *www.kavkazcenter.com/russ/content/2011/03/22/80140.shtml*.

112. See Hahn, *Russia's Islamic Threat*, pp. 221-25; and Gordon M. Hahn, "Anti-Americanism, Anti-Westernism, and Anti-Semitism Among Russia's Muslims," *Demokratizatsiya*, Vol. 16, No. 1, Winter 2008, pp. 49-60.

113. "Belgian Islamist Abou Imran, of Shariah4Belgium: We Will Conquer the White House, Europe Will Be Dominated by Islam," *MEMRI*, #2695, November 9, 2010, 09:42, available from *www.memritv.org/clip/en/2695.htm*.

114. Stephen Castle, "Police Arrest Suspects in Plot Against Belgium," *New York Times*, November 23, 2010, available from *www.nytimes.com/2010/11/24/world/europe/24belgium.html*; Philippe Siuberski, "Police arrest 11 over Belgium 'terror plot'," *Agence France Presse*, November 23, 2010, available from *news.yahoo.com/s/afp/20101123/wl_afp/belgiumnetherlandsgermany securityattacks/print*; and Philippe Siuberski, "Belgium arrests 26 in raids against terror," *NineMSN*, November 24, 2010, 06:13, available from *news.ninemsn.com.au/world/8168623/10-held-over-terror-plot-in-belgium*.

115. Valentina Pop, "Chechen Terror Suspects Busted in Belgian Raid," *EU Observer*, November 24, 2010, 09:29, available from *euobserver.com/9/31341*; and Olesya Khantsevich, "Chechenskoe podpol'e raskryto v Belgii," *Nezavsismaya gazeta*, November 25, 2010, available from *www.ng.ru/world/2010-11-25/1_belgium.html*.

116. Castle, "Police Arrest Suspects in Plot Against Belgium"; Siuberski, "Police arrest 11 over Belgium 'terror plot'"; Siuberski, "Belgium arrests 26 in raids against terror"; Pop, "Chechen Terror Suspects Busted in Belgian Raid"; and Khantsevich, "Chechenskoe podpol'e raskryto v Belgii."

117. "Austria arrests Chechen fugitive in Belgium plot," *AP*, December 4, 2010, 8:51:46, available from *www.themoscowtimes.com/news/article/austria-arrests-chechen-in-belgian-nato-plot/425658.html*.

118. "Austrian police arrest Chechen over possible jihad attack on Belgian NATO facility," *Jihad Watch*, December 4, 2010, available from *www.jihadwatch.org/2010/12/austrian-police-arrest-chechen-over-possible-jihad-attack-on-belgian-nato-base.html*; and "Austrian police hold Chechen in Belgian attack probe," *Expatica*, December 4, 2010, available from *www.expatica.com/be/news/belgian-news/austrian-police-hold-chechen-in-belgium-attack-probe_115126.html*, citing "Austrian police hold Chechen in Belgian attack probe," *Agence France Press*, December 4, 2010.

119. "Suspected Terrorist: A Ghost in Neunkirchen," *Die Presse*, December 5, 2010, 18:19, available from *diepresse.com/home/panorama/oesterreich/616045/Mutmasslicher-Terrorist_Ein-Phantom-in-Neunkirchen?direct=611111&_vl_backlink=/home/politik/innenpolitik/index.do&selChannel=100*.

120. "Qaeda Plans US, UK Christmas Attacks: Iraq Official," *Reuters*, December 16, 2010, 3:35, available from *www.reuters.com/article/2010/12/16/us-iraq-qaeda-idUSTRE6BF3CR20101216*.

121. "Obrashchenie musul'man Bel'gii k imamu Abu Mukhamammadu al'-Makdisi za naztavleniem," *Islamdin.com*, June 22, 2010, 19:01, available from *www.islamdin.com/index.php?option=com_content&view=article&id=814:2010-06-22-19-09-08&catid=25:2009-02-09-17-15-12&Itemid=17*.

122. Castle, "Police Arrest Suspects in Plot Against Belgium"; Siuberski, "Police arrest 11 over Belgium 'terror plot'"; and Siuberski, "Belgium arrests 26 in raids against terror."

123. "Czech Police Arrest Suspected Russia's North Caucasus Terrorists," *BNO News*, May 3, 2011, 2:27, available from *wireupdate. com/wires/17128/czech-police-arrest-suspected-russias-north-caucasus-terrorists/*.

124. "Policie stiha pet lidi z podpory terorismu," *Lydovki*, Prague, May 3, 2011, 11:19 and 16:15, available from *www.lidovky. cz/tiskni.asp?r=ln_domov&c=A110503_111957_ln_domov_ape*; and Christian Falvey, "Police uncover first case of a terrorist network operating in the Czech Republic, eight charged with aiding Dagestani Shariat Jamaat," *Radio Praha*, May 4, 16:24, available from *www.radio.cz/en/section/curraffrs/police-uncover-first-case-of-a-terrorist-network-operating-in-the-czech-republic-eight-charged-with-aiding-dagestani-shariat-jamaat*.

125. "Czech Police Arrest Suspected Russia's North Caucasus Terrorists."

126. "Nemetskaya politsiya arestovala grazhdanina RF po podozreniyu v prichastnosti k teraktam v Chechne i Dagestane," *Kavkaz uzel*, June 24, 2011, 7:10, available from *www.kavkaz-uzel.ru/articles/187809/*.

127. "Double anti-terrorist operation in Le Mans," *Lemans Maville*, July 5, 2010, available from *www.lemans.maville.com/actu/actudet_-Double-operation-antiterroriste-au-Mans-_dep-1440912_actu.Htm*.

128. "Doukaev far 12 ar for terror," *Avisen.dk*, May 31, 2011, 11:32, available from *avisen.dk/doukaev-faar-12-aar-for-terror_147226.aspx?utm_source=avisen&utm_medium=frontpage&utm_campaign=latestNewsBox*. In December 2010, Danish authorities brought charges against the ethnic Chechen, Lors Doukaev, for involvement in a terrorist plot. Doukaev, who lost a leg at age 12 due to an explosion in his native Chechnya, was arrested in September in a Copenhagen hotel after apparently he accidentally detonated an explosive device he was preparing. He was found with a map on which was the location of the offices of the newspaper *Jyllands-Posten*, which published the famous caricatures of the Prophet Mohammad in 2005. "Urozhentsu Chechni Dukaevu v Danii pred'yavleno obvinenie v terrorizme," *Kavkaz uzel*, December 21, 2010, 19:09, available from *www.kavkaz-uzel.ru/articles/178729/*.

129. See, for example, "Issledovanie o pravovom statuse ispol'zovaniya oruzhiya massovogo porazheniya protiv nevernykh," *Islamdin.com*, January 9, 2010.

130. Gordon M. Hahn, "The Bioterrorism Threat in the Russian Federation," in Rebecca Katz and Raymond A. Zilinskas, eds., *Encyclopedia of Bioterrorism Defense*, 2nd Ed., Hoboken, NJ: John Wiley and Sons, Inc., 2011, pp. 581-584.

131. "FSB Has Info On Terrorists Attempts To Seize Fissile Materials," *Itar-Tass*, June 2, 2010, available from *www.itar-tass.com*; and "Russia says terrorist seeking nuclear materials," *Reuters*, June 2, 2011, available from *www.reuters.com/article/2010/06/02/us-russia-security-nuclear-idUSTRE6512RQ20100602*.

132. For more details, see Gordon M. Hahn, "The *Jihadi* Insurgency and the Russian Counterinsurgency in the North Caucasus," *Post-Soviet Affairs*, Vol. 24, No. 1, January-February 2008, pp. 1-39.

133. A short list of top CE amirs killed over the last few years includes: at least six successive DV amirs (Vagabov, killed on August 10, 2010; 'Al-Bara' Umalat Magomedov, January 6, 2010; Nabi Mediddinov, 2009; 'Muaz' Omar Sheikhulaev, March 10, 2009; 'Muaz' Ilgar Mollachiev, February 5, 2009; Abdul Majid, October 1, 2007; the Algerian amir, Doctor Mohammed, August 31, 2009; Arab amir, Seif al-Islam al-Urdani, February 2, 2010; Buryatskii, March 4, 2010; Astemirov, March 24, 2010; Astemirov's successor as OVKBK amir, Arsen Tatarov, March 31, 2010; Galgaiche Vilaiyat (GV) naibs, Adam Korigov, April 9, 2010; and 'Shamil' Akhmed Tsaloev, April 9, 2010; North African amir, Yasir Amarat, June 8, 2010; Urus Martan Sector amir, 'Abdul Malik' Chingiskhan Gishaev, January 19, 2010; Vedeno Raion Sector amir, Ilman Istamirov, February 4, 2010; CE naib, Supyan Abduallayev, March 28, 2011; the Jordanian amir, Abu Anas Muhannad, May 2011; Groznyi Front amir, Hamzat Shemilev, August 23, 2010; GV amir, Ilez Gardanov, August 23, 2010; and six top OVKBK amirs, including the OVKBK's amir, vali Askar Dzhappuev, April 2011.

134. "Poslanie Federal'nomu Sobraniyu Rossiiskoi Federatsii," *Kremlin.ru*, November 12, 2009, 13:45, available from *www.kremlin.ru/transcripts/5979*; and Guy Falconbridge and Denis

Dyomkin, "N. Caucasus strife is Russia's top problem-Kremlin," *Reuters*, November 12, 2009.

135. Andrew C. Kuchins, Matthew Malarkey, and Sergey Markedonov, *The North Caucasus: Russia's Volatile Frontier*, A Report of the Russia and Eurasia Program, Washington, DC: Center for Strategic and International Studies, March 2011, available from *csis.org/files/publication/110321_Kuchins_North-Caucasus_WEB.pdf*; and Ivan Sukhov, "'Kuda eti den'gi delis'?'" *Moskovskie novosti*, April 4, 2011, 00:32, available from *mn.ru/politics/20110404/300841916.html*.

136. Tatyana Stanovaya, "Problemy Severnogo Kavkaza: Mezhdu Prezidenton and Pravitelstvom," *Politkom.ru*, August 8, 2011, available from *www.politcom.ru*.

137. *Ibid.*

138. Kuchins, Malarkey, and Markedonov, *The North Caucasus: Russia's Volatile Frontier*; and Sukhov, "'Kuda eti den'gi delis'?'"

139. "Na Severnom Kavkaze budet sozdano ne menee 400 tysyach rabochikh mest, Mezhregional'naya konferentsiya 'Yedinoi Rossii' 'Razvitie Kavkaza 2010-2012," Yedinaya Rossiya Website, July 7, 2010, available from *www.edinros.ru/text.shtml?14/4565,110040*; and Ivan Sukhov, "Semeinnyi podryad," *Vremya novostei*, July 7, 2010, *www.vremya.ru/2010/117/4/257340.html*.

140. *Ibid.*

141. Abu Amin, "'Investitsii' v Severnyi Kavkaz, ili popytka putinskoi svory ostanovit' protsess otdeleniya Severnogo Kavkaza ot rusni i stanovleniya na ego meste islamskogo gosudarstva Imarat Kavkaz," *Islamdin.com*, February 20, 2011.

142. "Na Severnom Kavkaze budet sozdano ne menee 400 tysyach rabochikh mest, Mezhregional'naya konferentsiya 'Yedinoi Rossii' 'Razvitie Kvkaza 2010-2012"; and Sukhov, "Semeinnyi podryad."

143. The project is being organized under a new open stock company North Caucasus Resorts (*Kurorty Severnogo Kavkaza*) headed by Akhmed Bilalov.

144. Timur Samedov, Musa Muradov and Khalim Aminov, "Boeviki otkryli vserossiiskii kurort," *Kommersant*, February 21, 2011, pp. 1, 3, available from *www.kommersant.ru/doc. aspx?DocsID=1589344*.

145. "Russia, France plan joint holiday resorts in turbulent North Caucasus," *RIA Novosti*, June 29, 2011, 08:02 AM PDT, available from *en.rian.ru/russia/20110629/164915641.html*.

146. "Yevkurov zaprosil dopolnitel'no 20 podrazdelenii spetsnaza GRU," January 4, 2010, 19:58, available from *kavkazcenter. com/russ/content/2010/01/04/69927.shtml*.

147. Sergei Minenko, "Al'-Kaida' na 'Zhigulyakh'," *Vremya novostei*, February 4, 2010, available from *www.vremya.ru/246760. html*; and "36 Fighters Voluntarily Surrendered in 2010," *Russia Eurasia Terrorism Watch*, November 7, 2010, available from *www. retwa.com/home.cfm?articleDate=7Nov2010*.

148. "Yevkurov predlagaet boevikam v Ingushetii sdat'sya v obmen na myagkoe nakazanie," *Kavkaz uzel*, February 9, 2010, 11:30, available from *www.kavkaz-uzel.ru/articles/165231/*.

149. *Ibid.*

150. "Prezident Ingushetii vstretilsya s rodstvennikami ukryvavshikh Saida Buryatskogo," *Kavkaz uzel*, March 7, 2010, 00:55, available from *www.kavkaz-uzel.ru/articles/166249/*.

151. Ivan Sukhov, "Kalymskii krai," *Vremya novostei*, July 8, 2010, available from *www.vremya.ru/2010/118/4/257507.html*.

152. Sukhov, "'Kuda eti den'gi delis?'"

153. "Yevkurov zaprosil dopolnitel'no 20 podrazdelenii spetsnaza GRU."

154. Hahn, "Comparing the Level of Caucasus Emirate Terrorist Activity in 2008 and 2009"; Hahn, "Trends in Jihadist Violence in Russia During 2010 in Statistics"; and Hahn, "CE-Affiliated Website Reports Number of Jihadi Attacks and Resulting Casualties from January Through June 2011."

155. RFERL Newsline, Vol. 11, No. 82, May 4, 2007.

156. "UFSB: v Kabardino-Balkarii sokhranyaetsya ugroza teraktov," *Kavkaz Memo*, March 15, 2007, available from *www. kavkaz.memo.ru/newstext/news/id/118554.html*.

157. RFERL Newsline, Vol. 11, No. 82, May 4, 2007.

158. Hahn, "Comparing the Level of Caucasus Emirate Terrorist Activity in 2008 and 2009"; Hahn, "Trends in Jihadist Violence in Russia During 2010 in Statistics"; and Hahn, "CE-Affiliated Website Reports Number of Jihadi Attacks and Resulting Casualties from January Through June 2011."

159. Kanokov emphasized that the new year was beginning "much worse than last year," a year in which the mujahedin killed "six times as many law enforcement personnel killed than in previous years." Sergei Polyakov, "Kabardino-Balkariya sprosit pomoshchi v bor'be s terroristami," *Infox.ru*, February 3, 2011, 17:46, available from *infox.ru/accident/incident/2011/02/03/ Kabardino_Balkariya_.phtml*.

160. "Shkhagoshev: terakt v Nalchike—pryamoe pokushenie na prezidenta Kabardino-Balkarii," *Kavkaz uzel*, May 4, 2010, 17:59, available from *kabardino-balkariya.kavkaz-uzel.ru/articles/168443/*.

161. "'Novyi kurs Magomedova'? Situatsii s pravami cheloveka i popytki konsolidatsii obshchestva v Respublike Dagestan. Fevralya 2010—mart 2011 g.," *Kavkaz uzel*, April 12, 2011, 11:54, available from *www.kavkaz-uzel.ru/articles/183646/?print=true, sections 7.1 and 7.2*.

162. Andrey Bondarev, "The President of Dagestan meets with the delegation of ZAO Russian Copper Company," *RIA Novosti*, May 13, 2011, 11:32, available from *www.riadagestan.com/ news/2011/05/13/6472/*.

163. Maksim Tivkailo, "Kerimov vlozhit v gostinitsy i sta-diony Dagestana $1.4 mlrd," *Vedomosti*, July 15, 2011, available from *www.vedomosti.ru/companies/news/1319006/kerimov_vlozhit_v_gostinicy_i_stadiony_dagestana_14_mlrd*.

164. Hahn, "Comparing the Level of Caucasus Emirate Ter-rorist Activity in 2008 and 2009"; Hahn, "Trends in Jihadist Vio-lence in Russia During 2010 in Statistics"; and Hahn, "CE-Affil-iated Website Reports Number of Jihadi Attacks and Resulting Casualties from January Through June 2011."

165. With regard to abductions in Dagestan, which are car-ried out most often but not always by authorities, there were 15 abductions, including four found dead and two found in police detention on average in the 3 years prior to Magomedov. Dur-ing Magomedov's first year, 2010, there were 18, including four found dead and seven found in police detention. See Table 1 in "Vvedenie" of "'Novyi kurs Magomedova'? Situatsii s pravami cheloveka i popytki konsolidatsii obshchestva v Respublike Dagestan. Fevralya 2010 – mart 2011 g."

166. On recent violations and European Court of Human Rights (ECHR) cases, see, for example, the Russian human rights organization Memorial's reports "Situatsiya v zone konflikta na Severnom Kavkaze: otsenka pravozashitnikov. Vesna 2011 g.," *Kavkaz uzel*, July 22, 2011, 00:00, available from *www.kavkaz-uzel.ru/articles/189517/#6*; and "'Novyi kurs Magomedova'? Situatsii s pravami cheloveka i popytki konsolidatsii obshchestva v Respub-like Dagestan. Fevralya 2010 – mart 2011 g," sections 5.1-5.6.

167. "V Dagestane sozdadut spetspodrazdelenie Vnutren-nykh voisk MVD," *Kavkaz uzel*, December 15, 2010, 15:45, avail-able from *www.kavkaz-uzel.ru/articles/174793/*; and "Dagestantsy dadut dostoiny otpor banditskomu otreb'yu," *Kavkaz news*, No-vember 11, 2010, 12:42, available from *www.kavkaz-news.info/portal/cnid_122389/alias__Caucasus-Info/lang__en/tabid__2434/de-fault.aspx*.

168. Marc Sageman, *Leaderless Jihad: Terrorism Networks in the Twenty-First Century*, Philadelphia, PA: University of Pennsylva-nia Press, 2008.

169. Robert A. Pape, *Dying to Win: The Strategic Logic of Suicide Terrorism*, New York: Random House, 2005. See also Robert A. Pape and James K. Feldman, *Cutting the Fuse: The Explosion of Global Suicide Terrorism and How to Stop It*, Chicago, IL: University of Chicago Press, 2010.

170. Rose revolution leaders and former Saakashvili allies, former parliament speaker Nino Burjanadze and former Defense Minister Irakly Okruashvili, have claimed that Tbilisi has been training Ingush mujahedin and that Georgian banks have facilitated money transfers to the Caucasus mujahedin. "Burjanadze Talks About Danger of one more War from Russia," *Georgian Journal*, October 21, 2010, available from *georgianjournal.ge/index. php?option=com_content&view=article&id=664:burjanadze-talks-about-danger-of-one-more-war-from-russia-&catid=9:news&Itemid=8*; and "Burjanadze Slams Visa Provocations," *Interfax*, October 21, 2010, 19:01, available from *www.interfax.com/newsinf. asp?pg=2&id=197175*. Former U.S. Foreign Service officer and U.S. Senate Republican Policy Committee foreign policy analyst, James George Jatras claims that in December 2009 a secret meeting took place in Tbilisi with "representatives of numerous jihad groups based in various Islamic and European countries for the purpose of coordinating their activities on Russia's southern flank." According to Jatras, "the meeting was organized under the auspices of high officials of the Georgian government." "In addition to 'military' operations, (i.e., attacks in southern Russia) special attention was given to ideological warfare, for example, launching of the Russian-language TV station 'First Caucasus'." James Jatras, "The Georgian Imbroglio—And a Choice for the United States," *America-Russia Net*, February 14, 2010, available from *www.america-russia.net/eng/face/236661338?user_session=4827 e878c0267ddbdd6ee738f8212f1d*.

CHAPTER 2

THE NORTH CAUCASUS IN RUSSIA AND RUSSIA IN THE NORTH CAUCASUS: STATE APPROACHES AND POLITICAL DYNAMICS IN THE TURBULENT REGION

Sergey Markedonov

Any attempts to make generalizations about Russian policy on the North Caucasus face serious methodological difficulties. In spite of analysts' personal attitude to the problem, all observers agree that this area is the most acute one in Russia. Here the problem of Russia's territorial integrity and sustainability is being resolved.

The growth of political violence (the most impressive example is the tragic terrorist bombing at Moscow's Domodedovo International Airport in January 2011) has brought the danger of growing instability in the region to the attention of foreign countries, especially on the eve of the Sochi Olympics of 2014 and World Soccer Cup of 2018. While in the 1990s violence in the North Caucasus was primarily based in Chechnya, over the last years it has increased for other republics like Dagestan, Ingushetia, and Kabardino-Balkaria (KBR). The North Caucasus agenda today is extremely tense with the events and challenges of terrorism and counterterrorism. In 2009, the counterterrorist operation (CTO) regime in Chechnya was cancelled, but in 2010 there was not only a quantitative but also qualitative rise in the attacks in this republic (like the attack on Tsentoroy, the native village of Ramzan Kadyrov, as well as that of the Chechen parliament in Grozny). At the same time, violence in the neighboring republics (Dagestan, Ingushetia, and KBR) has not declined either. In 2010, KBR, which had a reputation of being a "Sleeping Beauty" during the 1990s surpassed Chechnya in the number of acts of terrorism, taking a place in the top three, after Dagestan and Ingushetia, with 48 explosions, 21 shootings, and 14 attempts on the life of law enforcement officials and special troops. During the same period, local CTOs were launched twice in the republic, with the operation in Tyrnauza lasting from October 20 through December 25. For the first time in the recent history of North Caucasus terrorism, there was an attack on an industrial facility in 2010: targeted at the Baksan Hydroelectric Plant in KBR.[1] Almost every day, sabotage and terrorist attacks on representatives of law enforcement and military personnel take place along with civilian murders. We can also observe the revival of ethnic nationalism (despite the fact that radical Islamism has not handed over its positions, rather, on the contrary, it has grown), and at the same time, we see a fundamentally important step to resolving long-standing ethno-political confrontation between North Ossetia and Ingushetia. The struggle for power inside the Caucasus constituencies repeatedly makes itself felt through corrupt, authoritarian, and even occasionally violent means.

Apart from the growing violence that plagues the region, the Caucasus has become a subject of great importance in Russia. This thesis was proven by the events on Manege Square in December 2010 and increasing interethnic clashes between Russians and Caucasian peoples (Chechens and Dagestanis).[2] This is becoming a serious issue. Interestingly, the phenomenon of Russian ethnic chauvinism directed against the peoples of the Caucasus has recently assumed a macro-economic veneer. In April 2011, the Russian Civil Union movement organized a rally in Moscow under the slogan: "Stop feeding the Caucasus."[3] Participants objected to the federal government subsidizing its counterparts in Chechnya, Dagestan, and other republics, likening the North Caucasus to "a voracious crocodile which demands more blood and money." This problem could become more serious if the Russian officials attempt to exploit these ideas. We can already see attempts to use anti-Caucasus public opinion to obtain additional popularity on the eve of both parliamentary and presidential elections.[4]

However, Russian policy in the region has not really been conceptualized or even verbalized, and this circumstance creates many obstacles (first and foremost for Russian authorities) for adequately comprehending what Moscow wants to do. There is a great paradox in this situation. Identifying itself as a guarantor of Caucasus stability and security and demonstrating its willingness to pretend to be a key stakeholder for the whole region, including newly independent and de facto states of the South Caucasus, Russia faces challenges inside its own country regarding the North Caucasus area. Moreover, in 2009 the situation there was characterized as the most important domestic policy issue by President Dmitry Medvedev in his Presidential Address to the Federal Assembly (Parliament).[5] As a result, the Kremlin and the federal government brought in an official position of special plenipotentiary — with broadened functions in the newly created North Caucasus Federal District. For the first time in Russia's post-Soviet history, this official has the rank of deputy prime-minister.

In this chapter, some basic aspects will be considered. To what extent has recognition of the systemic and internal natures of the North Caucasus challenges helped to change political dynamics in the region? Why has the activity of the new plenipotentiary not been effective and failed to reach expectations? What new challenges would define the agenda in the most turbulent area of Russia? The purpose of this report is to examine major social and political trends in the North Caucasus region, with an emphasis on the last 3 years because historical aspects (including the 1990s) are separate topics for discussion.

"SOFT POWER": MADE BY ALEXANDER KHLOPONIN

In the early 2000s, the Russian authorities were all too ready to speak about the North Caucasus. Discussion centered on several topics. The first was the Caucasus as a platform for international terrorism, where Russia was being put to the test. The image of the "international terrorist" changed according to the political situation of the time. Sometimes the face had Georgian features, at other times Afghan and sometimes even the "treacherous West" seemed to be involved. The role of the West in affairs of the North Caucasus was actually interpreted in two ways. On the one hand, the West was seen as a natural ally at risk from Third World intrigues, and on the other, an unimaginative and bothersome partner trying to impose its incorrect ideas (or "double standards") upon Russia. The second topic was the swiftly stabilizing Caucasus, an image that effectively came to mean Chechnya under the wise leadership of Akhmad and then Ramzan Kadyrov, father and son. There were attempts to diversify the North Caucasus issue: The most outstanding examples were the speeches by

Dmitry Kozak, the Russian President's representative in the South (in this position from September 2004 to September 2007). He tried to focus the attention of his immediate superiors and society on the problems of the clan system and the inefficiency of the regional administrations (particularly in conditions of budget dependency on the federal centre). However, Russia's ruling elite was not concerned with the region's domestic situation, at least until the middle of 2011.

The decision to end CTO in Chechnya in April 2009, dictated as it was by public relations considerations, did not have the effect of reducing the number of terrorist acts in that republic. Diversionary terrorist activity actually spread to the neighboring republics of Dagestan and Ingushetia. That summer saw a brazen attempt to assassinate Ingushetia's president Yunus-Bek Yevkurov, which temporarily put him out of action. Aldigirei Magomedtagirov, Interior Minister of Dagestan, the largest North Caucasus republic, was murdered. All this required some coherent explanation. It was impossible just to keep saying that the region would soon be stabilized, although "some people are working against this."

Medvedev's Makhachkala speech on June 9, 2009, marked the moment when the focus changed from external to internal threats. The Russian President talked of "systemic problems" in the North Caucasus region. For the first time since the 1990s, the head of state was officially admitting that socio-political turbulence in the Russian Caucasus was not the result of foreign interference, but of internal problems like corruption, unemployment, and poverty. However, both the President and the Prime Minister still kept talking about the battle with "bandits" and "organized crime groups," as if the current problems of the Caucasus could be compared to the situation in Harlem, New York, or Southeast Washington, DC, in the 1980s. The failures of government in the North Caucasus were not honestly discussed. Blame was laid on the regional and local authorities, while the federal authorities escaped criticism. This was the origin of bizarre ideas like the introduction of special jurisdiction for matters involving terrorism. Regardless, in his address last year, Medvedev called the North Caucasus the main problem of Russian domestic politics. That was when another idea emerged: a new bureaucratic structure, backed by Medvedev and Vladimir Putin, entrusted with "establishing order" in the North Caucasus.

As a result, Alexander Khloponin arrived in the Caucasus in January 2010 as Moscow's plenipotentiary. This looked like an innovation. The man responsible for Russia's most unstable region was not one of the siloviki (members of the central bureaucracy), but a manager who had worked for "Norilsk Nickel" enterprise and served as governor of the Taymyr Peninsula and Krasnoyarsk. The media adopted a different language when discussing the North Caucasus. Apart from the usual reference to "terrorists" and "extremists," they began talking of "clusters," "investments," and "innovations."

But Khloponin's appointment had nothing to do with modernization. It was a typical behind-the-scenes advancement of a person lacking the appropriate experience, motivated by internal bureaucratic logic, rather than pressing national interest. In addition, the functions of this new head of the Caucasus were very limited. Khloponin was thrown in the deep end of the pool, without being given the necessary political powers to keep himself afloat. And how can there be any real investment or innovation in a region so close to a state of war? In the end, things did not turn out for the better, but as usual, as Viktor Chernomyrdin so memorably put it in 1993: "We wanted the best but it came out like it always does."

The economy and the social sphere were recognized as important. The Kremlin and the Federal Government put all their efforts into developing these sectors, but political themes (ethnic conflicts and the relations between the different religions) remained taboo. They were seen as merely superficial, a function of the socio-economic situation. This has made it impossible to produce a large-scale strategy for the development of the Caucasus. When the politics of the region are as unstable as they are, socio-economic conditions matter, but while unquestionably important, they do not play a determining role.

Still, on July 6, 2010, Putin asked for a strategy document to be delivered "within a period of 2 months," a reasonable amount of time for a good academic article or a chapter of a book, but not for a document with a 15-year perspective. By September 6, 2010, the draft of the strategy was ready. In less than a month, it went through the entire cycle from being signed to publication by the federal government. The aims and objectives of "Strategy-2025," as set out in the initial "General Provisions," are skewed from the very beginning. We read that:

> The Strategy takes account of:
> - The current state of the economy of Russian Federation administrative entities which are part of The North Caucasus Federal District;
> - The Russian economy;
> - The global economy;
> - Their potential for development; and,
> - Regional and inter-regional projects and their outcomes.[6]

But what about the political development of the Caucasus? Don't the facts of terrorism, subversive actions, and an ethnocratic leadership automatically make any business plan a "risky undertaking"? Shouldn't future investors be taking this into account (unless the money comes from the federal budget, which does not depend on public opinion)?

> The North Caucasus District offers favorable conditions for developing the agro-industrial complex, the spheres of tourism and health tourism, electricity, mining and manufacturing. It also affords developed transit facilities. However, economic and socio-political instability mean that natural advantages remain unrealized and make the North Caucasus Federal District an unattractive environment for investment.[7]

The political element is mentioned in passing, after the economy, and is not elaborated upon in any way. What does socio-political instability mean? Is it the separatist threat or the "religious revival" which is incompatible with the constitutional and legal regulations and laws of the Russian Federation? According to Strategy-2025, "The main goal of the Strategy is to provide conditions conducive to the rapid growth of the real sector of the economy in Russian Federation administrative units that make up the North Caucasus Federal District. Also to create new jobs, and improve the standard of life." What a wonderful goal! But is this possible in an area that is practically on a war footing (This is the felicitous description of the present situation given by the head of the Prosecutor General's Office Investigative Committee Alexander Bastrykin in an interview with radio "Moscow Echo")[8]? It is not the grey economy, which makes its living from illegal or semi-legal deals, that is being discussed in this document. Incidentally, Strategy-2025 does not set itself to deal with institutional change, i.e. creating a new generation of managers who could give the economy the chance to breathe without killing it with their kickbacks and pay-offs. The abuse of power and illegal methods of carrying out anti-terrorist operations give rise to a lack of trust in the authorities, and even a situation where people start regarding law enforcers as enemies. Young people who are constantly victimized become particularly vulnerable to recruitment by the rebels. There is plenty of evidence that the activity of the armed underground has been growing recently. The crisis will only get worse if the state keeps fighting the insurgents using methods like kidnapping and executions without trial. Two incomplete subsections of Strategy-2025 are devoted to ethnic relations, but they are limited to generalities. There is no real information and no analysis. "The current socio-political and ethno-political situation in the North Caucasus Federal District is characterized by several pronounced negative social tendencies, manifestations of ethno-political and religious extremism, and a high risk of conflict."[9]

Any specialist could probably find a great many negative tendencies in any part of the Russian Federation, if he or she so desired. They exist in Moscow and St. Petersburg (Is not xenophobia a "negative social tendency"?), and in the Volga area (where there is both ethnic and religious extremism). But the difference between the Caucasus and the Volga area is that only in the North Caucasus is there a situation akin to war. This document of considerable strategic importance offers no explanation for why events developed as they did. The reader is left to guess. The

Strategy's analytical section does not even have a sub-section dealing with the religious revival, although radical Islam is the main vehicle for protests in the Caucasus. Anything to do with relations between the religions is relegated to the subsection "Ethnic Relationships." The reasons for the growth of radical Islam are set out with alarming simplicity: "Radical forms of Islam (have been) imported into the said Federal District." The text offers no explanation as to what these "imported forms" are, why they have been imported into the region, what the expectations of the importers are, or the extent to which the importers have gained indigenous support.[10] In the interests of objectivity, one can say, of course, that other reasons for the dissemination of extremist views (the Strategy makes no special distinction between nationalists and Islamists) include "widespread corruption" or "questions relating to the owning and disposing of land, which are unregulated and the cause of most of the ethnic conflicts, including at the level of the man in the street," and also "ethnic tension as a result of ill-defined civic identity."[11] But again, none of this can be linked to the need for institutional change in the Caucasus. In short, the objectives of "Strategy-2025" are clearly unachievable. It focuses on economic growth without addressing the socio-political preconditions that make the North Caucasus explosive and unstable. This document seems to isolate the economy and the social sphere from the rest of the complex whole.

NORTH CAUCASUS: RADICAL ISLAMISM
ON THE RISE

Since the Beslan tragedy in September 2004, the main anti-Russian discourse in the North Caucasus has not been under the slogans of ethno-political self-determination but under the green banner of radical Islam. On October 31, 2007, President of the so-called "Chechen Republic of Icheria," Doku Umarov, built upon his powers as the head of the separatist government and proclaimed a new formation — the Caucasus Emirate (CE).

Umarov proclaimed himself as "the only legitimate authority in all areas where there are Mujahideen." He also said that he denies the laws of the secular authorities that exist in the North Caucasus. It is hard to define Umarov personally and many of his supporters as real Islamists in the fullest sense of the word; they lack the necessary theological training and, in some cases, elementary education base. But for such unskilled Islamists the ideals of "pure Islam" are the main drivers of protest activities against the Russian State. With them, they have to determine the effectiveness of its potential for mobilizing extremists. To some extent, belonging to a radical Islamist current is a marker of radicalism in general (ethnic nationalism in this context is regarded as a moderate political movement that could include dialogue and certain concessions to the Russian State).

However, at the same time, we can report the presence in the ranks of the North Caucasian Islamists trained preachers who fully meet the standards of "Mujahedin of the future" (that is competent theologians, who could exploit both explosives and Kalashnikovs). The most famous of them were not ethnic

Chechens by origin. In 2009 they came to the forefront in the Caucasus radical Islamist movement. They brought new characters into the anti-Russian struggle in the North Caucasus. It is unlikely that such a man as Said Buryatskii (1982-2010, a.k.a. Alexander Tikhomirov, on his father's side a Buryat and on his mother's side a Russian) could inspire the defenders of a secular nationalist project to fight. Rather his appeal was religious.

In June 2009, Umarov's supporters claimed responsibility for the murder of the interior minister of Dagestan, Adilgerei Magomedtagirov as well as murders of Aza Gazgireeva, deputy Chairman of the Supreme Court of Ingushetia, and Bashir Aushev, former Deputy Prime Minister of Ingushetia. In July 2009, they announced their involvement in the attempted assassination of the President of Ingushetia, Yunus-Bek Yevkurov. In August, 2009, they issued a statement saying that the "accident" at the Sayano-Shushenskaya power plant was a matter of their hands. In November-December 2009, militants claimed responsibility for the murder of an Orthodox priest, Father Daniel (Sysoev) and the explosion of the train "Nevsky Express." On March 31, 2010, in his video address, Doku Umarov talked about his own orders for the suicide bombing in the Moscow subway, carried out on March 29. In January 2011, he claimed credit for the Domodedovo Airport terrorist attack.

Even if the responsibility for one or another of these attacks is not true, and is part of a public relations campaign, the struggle for "true faith" is selling and becoming a popular political commodity. This product will be even more in demand than would be the level of social injustice, judicial, and administrative efficiency. The aforementioned Buryatskii is a phenomenon in this regard. Not being a preacher from Pakistan or Arab countries, he found a fertile environment in the Caucasian audience as a result of his own religious and political evolution. Note that nowadays this audience knows the Soviet and Russian reality far less than what Jokhar Dudayev and Aslan Maskhadov did. The works of Sheikh Anwar al-Awlaki, Sheikh Abu Muhammed al-Maqdisi, and others feature prominently on various web portals associated with the Caucasus rebels. The Caucasus rebels have indeed embraced the political lexicon of the "global jihad," styling their leaders as "amirs" and establishing a "Caucasus Emirate" with its own "Shariah Court." It is much less connected with the nationwide socio-cultural environment. However, while assessing the "Islamic factor" it is necessary to add some nuances. Often many stories regarding the intra-administrative-bureaucratic struggle are hidden under the "Wahhabis" (as the Russian media define radical Islam). It would seem that the authorities both at regional and federal levels must do their utmost to understand where there are religious radicals or simple criminals, and where their synthesis takes place (the latter is extremely important to discredit the militants and their ideological patrons). But instead of doing this, officials repeat propaganda theses about the "agonizing bandits."

ETHNIC NATIONALISM: NEW PERSPECTIVES?

The last 3 years showed, among other things, that the hope of "self-liquidation" of nationalism has not been justified. Rallies of Balkars and Circassians, interethnic relations in Dagestan and tensions between Ossets and Ingushsis forced the authorities to pay attention to the problem, which by the early 2000s had seemed generally to be clearing up. A revival of ethnic nationalism in the North Caucasus has taken place since 2008. For this development, there are both internal and external prerequisites. The Circassian issue revival has occurred after a series of personnel decisions of the fourth president of Karachaevo-Cherkessiya Republic (KCR), Boris Ebzeev. Russia's recognition of Abkhazia's independence on August 26, 2008, also played a role in the revitalization of Circassian ethnic nationalism as well as the upcoming Sochi Olympic Games. Since 2010, the "Circassian question" has become one of the focal points of the Georgian foreign policy agenda. Two conferences (March and November 2010), began the discussion at the parliamentary level of the problem of the so-called "Circassian genocide" in the Russian Empire in the 19th century, and finally Georgian recognition of this massacre as a case of genocide in May 2011 created a serious precedent. Before it, Russian policy in the Caucasus was not recognized as genocide by foreign states. This charge therefore contributes to the internationalization of debates about this troubled Russian region. Thus it requires from the Russian government and society more thoughtful action. Moscow must find competent answers to this problem as soon as possible.

However, the "new" nationalists in their statements remain within the Russian political-legal space. Balkars, the Ingush human rights activists, and Circassian activists are trying to appeal to the Federal Russian government, and not to the Council of Europe, the Parliamentary Assembly of the Council of Europe (PACE), or the European Union (EU)/United States. In March 2010, at a meeting dedicated to the 66th anniversary of the Russian deportation — of Balkars, Karachais, Chechens, Ingush, and Kalmyks to Siberia — the representatives of the Council of Elders of the Balkar people prepared an appeal to the presidential envoy in the North Caucasus Alexander Khloponin.

It is necessary to make a distinction between nationalism in the period of the "parade of sovereignties" in the early 1990s, and that of 2009-10. "The old nationalism" was a political riposte to the Soviet (and to a lesser extent the imperial) era. The current Balkar or Circassian movements, though using the historical material, have another nature. This is the reaction to today's realities (e.g., land issues and the attendant corruption, human resource policies, and issues of local self-government). Using quantitative approaches (and certain of their manifestations we see in KBR in the form of conciliation of the national movements) the danger of nationalism's revival can be minimized (but not eliminated completely). However (and 2009-2010 have demonstrated it), there are cases when the republican authorities try to extinguish the fire of Islamist activity by using nationalist kerosene. Such a tool (playing the ethnic card) is extremely dangerous (as shown in 1989-91).

The Ossetian-Ingush reconciliations have inspired cautious optimism. The third President of Ingushetia, Yunus Bek Evkurov, has played a great role in its promotion. Ingushetia now insists on the return of displaced persons who fled their homes during the conflict in October-November 1992, namely in the villages of the Suburban District (Prigorodnyi rayon) where they lived before the conflict, but the Ingush leadership clearly rejects the claims for the return of the district itself! At a meeting on the problems of displaced persons held on October 2, 2009, the President of North Ossetia, Teimuraz Mamsurov, said that the

Ingush would be free to return to the Suburban District and the authorities of his republic, North Ossetia, would not be an obstacle.

According to various sources, approximately 15-20,000 displaced people (DP) could return to their former places of residence. In this case, both the conflicting parties are dissatisfied with federal policy to resolve this problem. The Ossetian side said that the return of the Ingush is being done at a forced pace, while the Ingush are unhappy with the low intensity of the return. Soft apartheid is preserved. In particular, on March 1, 2009, during the elections of local bodies in the Suburban District, the vote was conducted in the villages settled by the Ingushis. The situation for all these years is complicated by the conflict between Georgia and South Ossetia because North Ossetia was forced to place Ossetian refugees from South Ossetia and interior regions of Georgia in its territory. Regardless of this, on December 17, 2009, the leaders of the two republics of Ingushetia and North Ossetia signed a bilateral agreement.

For the first time in the post-Soviet era Ingush DPs had the right to return to their homes in an official document. (Previously they were offered different versions of arrangements at the new location.) Human and civil rights took precedence over the "right of blood." Practically for the first time since 1992, it was recognized that the Ossetians and the Ingush are two peoples of the Russian nation-state project that should be more than just neighbors, and become fellow citizens of one country.

NORTH CAUCASUS: PUBLIC POLICY
OF LIMITED DURATION

In addition to Islam and ethnic nationalism, bureaucratic competition for dominance in the framework of a single republic has been a serious challenge. This management struggle has once again proved that disputes over power are not maintained in rigid adherence to an ethnic or religious affiliation. This is a complex configuration of clan interests and pressure groups both in Moscow and within the region itself. Perhaps the most exemplary republic in this respect is Dagestan, the largest (in territory and population) of the North Caucasian republics. It is no accident because the year of 2009 was a preparatory period for the Republican presidential elections (in February 2010, the Presidential term of Mukhu Aliev expired). In the absence of direct elections of the Republic's president, we witnessed complex bureaucratic fights with very specific ideas about public policy.

As a result, the procedure for determining a candidate for the presidency in Dagestan unprecedentedly dragged on from November 2009 until February 2010. In fact, it took 2 additional weeks beyond the legal procedure for Moscow to announce the final decision on the candidacy of the head of the Republic. Finally, Magomedsalam Magomedov got the support of the Federal Center. But as the Russian political scientist and journalist Ivan Sukhov justly remarked, "[The] appointment of the president in Dagestan looked like the most problematic one for the entire period."[12]

THE NORTH CAUCASUS FROM THE PERSPECTIVE OF THE KREMLIN

At first glance, the tragic events at the Manege Square on December 11, 2010 (and their echoes in St. Petersburg and Rostov-on-Don), are not connected directly with ethno-political and religious dynamics. Activity, clashes, and pogroms under the Russian ethno-nationalist slogans are not a response to one or another act of terrorism, sabotage, or injustice to the ethnic Russians in the North Caucasus republics. The Manege incident was provoked by the murder of Spartak soccer club fan Yegor Sviridov. In other cases, reasons are different, but they do not refer to the North Caucasus regional issues. Meanwhile, it would be very naïve to consider those clashes as absolutely isolated problems. The Sviridov case became a kind of trigger for anti-Caucasus opinions existing in the central parts of Russia. It also showed that Russia lacks a coherent national policy (or rather, it substituted folklore and ethnographic considerations) and that the inhabitants of the Caucasus and the rest of Russia had long lists of grievances against each other. Regardless of what it was, it revitalized the problem of a divided community and actualized the necessity to find ways for a civic nation option. It also demonstrated the challenge of Russian separatism because it displayed numerous groups of Russian citizens who would be ready to separate from the Caucasus. This fact violates the stereotype that the region can only be put beyond Moscow's strategic influence by means of a conscious campaign to free itself of Russia's suzerainty. But what if the unilateral separation of the Caucasus by Russian power took place? In this scenario, it would matter little whether the North

Caucasus followed a nationalist or Islamist agenda. It does not mean that Russia would have great benefits from the realization of this scenario. But now it has created new options for Caucasus politics as well as Russian domestic policy as a whole. The fact that the central government on the eve of the election year decided to play the Russian chauvinist bargaining chip is also dangerous because it makes two groups of the citizens of one country (ethnic Russians and Caucasus peoples) confront each other.

Thus, the North Caucasus has not become a more secure, and most importantly, predictable region. The region poses for the Russian state and society a wide variety of challenges, ranging from Islamic radicalism to sophisticated closed bureaucratic confrontation and Russian separatism. Despite the fact that in 2009 the Russian central government had recognized the crisis in the North Caucasus, breakthrough strategies for the development of the region have not surfaced. The state bodies continue focusing on bureaucratic methods of improving the situation, refuse to be engaged in dialogue with the civil society, and use "soft power" (integration projects, the introduction of elements of civic identity, and attempts to redefine the religious sphere such as "Euro-Islam" as an alternative to radical Islamism) in promoting their own interests. While modernization has been proclaimed as the strategic goal of the Russian policy, the North Caucasus has not been meaningfully considered in this context. By inertia, it is regarded rather as an underdeveloped outskirt, rather than an integral part of the nationwide political-legal space. Encouragingly, there is some safety margin; the region's population is interested in strengthening the Russian state's presence and the effectiveness of arbitration by the central government, while there is simultaneously a more active desire of the Russian authorities to make a critical assessment of the regional realities. However, an ad hoc situational response remains the dominant political and managerial style of the Russian elite for the Caucasus region.

ENDNOTES - CHAPTER 2

1. Sergey Markedonov, "Causes of the Growing Instability in Kabardino-Balkaria and Ways of Overcoming It," *Anthropology and Archeology of Eurasia*, Vol. 49, No. 4, 2011, pp. 72-81.

2. See our comment in *"Russian Separatism"* *("Russkii Separatizm")*, December, 16, 2010, available from *www.politcom.ru/11193. html*.

3. The Russian Civil Union is a public organization founded in November 2010. Ideologically it is based on alleged "national-democracy" principles. It seeks to give the ethnic Russians the right of self-determination and replace the federation in the Russian national democratic state.

4. Dmitry Rogozin, Russia's envoy to NATO, in his presentation, "National question in Russia and in Europe" for the Yaroslavl' World Forum, September 2011, identified the "Russian issue" as a core problem of Russia's domestic policy in the Caucuses and claimed a need to stop discrimination of ethnic Russians by the Caucasus peoples. Vladimir Putin (Russian prime-minister) in one of his speeches on December, 21, 2010, said: "We will have to develop the rules of registration in Moscow and Saint Petersburg as well as other big cities." It is worth noting that the practice of registration is an unconstitutional requirement because the Russian Constitution gives to all citizens the right of free movement.

5. Presidential Address to the Federal Assembly, The Kremlin, Moscow, Russia, November 12, 2009, available from *www. kremlin.ru/transcripts/5979*.

6. Strategy for the Socio-economic Development of the North Caucasus Federal District until 2025, July 6, 2010, available from *premier.gov.ru/events/news/13920/*.

7. *Ibid.*

8. This evaluation was done in the open air of the radio "Moscow Echo" [Ekho Moskvy], October, 10, 2010, available from *www.echo.msk.ru/news/717094-echo.html.*

9. Strategy for the Socio-economic Development of the North Caucasus Federal District until 2025.

10. *Ibid.*

11. *Ibid.*

12. Cited in "Kremlin Does not Comment on Delay with the Dagestan President appointment" ["Kreml' ne kommentiruet zaderzhku naznacheniya Prezidenta Dagestana"], January, 20, 2010, available from *www.kavkaz-uzel.ru/articles/164449/.*

CHAPTER 3

THE "AFGHANIZATION" OF THE NORTH CAUCASUS: CAUSES AND IMPLICATIONS OF A CHANGING CONFLICT

Svante E. Cornell

The situation in the North Caucasus, particularly in Chechnya, frequently made headlines in the 1990s and early 2000s. In fact, it was a key issue in affecting Western views of Russia, a particular mobilizing factor for the democracy and human rights agenda as Russia was concerned. This changed, however, with President Vladimir Putin's successful curtailing of media freedoms in Russia, and the gradual decline of violence in Chechnya, with violence sinking to a low point in 2006. For the past 5 years, the North Caucasus has hardly had an effect on relations between the West and Russia; in fact, both the media and policy communities in the West have largely ignored the region. That has nevertheless begun to change in the recent past, for two main reasons: First, there has been a clear upsurge in violence in and related to the North Caucasus since 2007, with the completion of the process of transformation of a Chechen nationalist rebellion to a region-wide Islamist insurgency. It has become clear that far from pacifying the region, Moscow is failing to exert sovereignty there. Second, the International Olympic Committee's decision to hold the 2014 Olympic Games in Sochi on the Russian Black Sea coast adjacent to the North Caucasus has made the North Caucasus a magnet for attention. This chapter seeks to assess the current situation in the North Caucasus, the reasons behind the evolution of the past decade, and its implications for Russia, the region, and the West.

THE NORTH CAUCASUS TODAY

The republics of the North Caucasus are presently characterized by a combination of factors that the present author has likened to "Afghanization." The term evokes the development of Afghanistan in the mid-1990s: a combination of war, human suffering, poverty, organized crime, and externally sponsored Islamic radicalism combined to generate an explosive situation, which the authorities are increasingly unable to respond to—and which, failing to understand the web of problems correctly and suffering from the constraints of their own system, they end up exacerbating.

Demographically and economically, the North Caucasus is in a deep malaise. Unemployment rates are sky-high, averaging 50 percent by some estimates, with 80 percent rates of youth unemployment being common in many areas of the region.[1] Between 60 and 90 percent of the budgets of the republics consist of direct subsidies from Moscow, suggesting the weakness of economic activity and of government ability to raise revenues. In fact, subsidies to the North Caucasus have begun to generate a backlash in Russia itself, with growing popular movements wanting to stop the government from "feeding the Caucasus."[2] A leaked Russian government report in 2006 cited that the shadow economy constituted an estimated 44 percent of Dagestan's economy, as opposed to 17 percent in Russia as a whole; 50 to 70 percent of Dagestanis with some form of employment were thought to work in the shadow economy.[3] These figures are unlikely to have improved since then. Ethnic Russians have largely left the region, removing some of the most-skilled labor force. In Chechnya, where 200,000 Russians once lived, they now number in the hundreds. In Ingushetia, the number of Russians declined by a factor of over six. In other republics, the decline between the censuses of 1989 and 2002 are not as dramatic but nevertheless stark: The percentage of Russians fell from 42 percent to 33 percent in Karachaevo-Cherkessiya; from 30 to 23 percent in North Ossetia; and from 10 to 5 percent in Dagestan. The exodus of Russians has only continued since then, although census figures are not available.[4] Meanwhile, the educational system has largely collapsed while there is a rapid population increase due to historically high birth rates.

Since 2004, with the strengthening of the "vertical of power" in Russia, the republics are ruled increasingly by elites whose main feature is loyalty (of an often personal nature) to the leadership in Moscow rather than, as had been the case, with roots in the local politics of the region. This has been a source of additional friction between Moscow and the populations of the North Caucasus. Not only are these populations no longer able to elect their leaders even on paper, but their leaders are responsive mainly to the demands of the distant capital rather than their own needs. While the most well-known example is Chechnya, where Moscow supported the elevation of the Kadyrov clan to lead the republic, the most egregious case is Ingushetia. There, a highly respected but independent-minded leader, General Ruslan Aushev, managed to keep the republic stable and peaceful during the first Chechen war and its chaotic aftermath. Deemed too independent, he was replaced in 2002 by a Federal Security Service (FSB) officer of Ingush descent but with little connection to the region, Murad Zyazikov. Zyazikov's subsequent mismanagement, insensitivity to local power-brokers, and repression alienated considerable parts of the population and led numerous young Ingush to join the armed resistance. Kabardino-Balkaria (KBR), Putin similarly appointed a Moscow-based businessman with roots in the republic, Arsen Kanokov, to the presidency in 2005, with the explicit purpose of appointing a person without links to the "clan politics" of the republic. However, Kanokov's lack of a popular base in KBR led the situation to deteriorate further.[5]

The North Caucasus is no longer the scene of large-scale warfare concentrated in Chechnya, as was the case in 1994-96 and 1999-2002. Instead, the resistance has morphed into a low-to-medium level insurgency that spans the entire region. Chechnya is among the calmer areas of the region, with the epicenter of the resistance having moved first to Ingushetia, then to Dagestan, with spikes of violence in KBR and the other republics as well. The conflict pits Moscow and its local allies, such as the Kadyrov clan, against loosely coordinated multiethnic groups of insurgents that largely remain led by ethnic Chechens. This insurgency no longer sees itself as a nationalist movement, but as part of the global jihadi movement. As such, it seeks the establishment of a region-wide Islamic state, dubbed the "Caucasus Emirate." Inspired by the global jihadi movement, the insurgency targets not only Russian forces but also civilian authorities across the region, as well as engaging in terrorist attacks on civilians, including in Russia proper. Thus, Chechnya has come to resemble Kashmir: a formerly nationalist and separatist insurgency morphed into a jihadi movement with whom central authorities can no longer, realistically, expect to reach a political compromise.

HOW DID WE GET HERE?

The present condition of the conflict in the North Caucasus is a fairly recent development, having undergone deep transformations in the past decade. An overview of the history of the conflict makes this clear. Indeed, it suggests that in 1989, ethnicity was increasingly politicized across the former Soviet Union. The ethno-nationalist uprisings and movements of 1989-94 clearly provide corroboration for that assessment. By contrast, religion was not politicized, and would not be for another decade. Among North Caucasus ethnic groups, only the Chechens had both the incentives and the capacity to sustain an insurgency against the Russian state, while a religious revival gradually got under way, centered on Dagestan. It was the first war in Chechnya in 1994-96 that attracted militant Islamist groups to the North Caucasus, whose ideology came to spread across the region, fanning out from Chechnya and Dagestan to span the North Caucasus.

The Salience of the Deportations.

The resistance of Chechens as well as other North Caucasian peoples to Russian rule in the 19th century is legendary. It is instructive to note that Russia had annexed Georgia by 1801, and acquired control over Armenia and Azerbaijan gradually in 1812-13 and 1827-28. By contrast, the areas north of the mountains were not subjugated until 1859-64. It took Russia 30 years after gaining control over the South Caucasus to pacify the North. Chechens, Dagestanis, and the Circassian peoples to the west fought an unequal battle until the 1860s to escape Russian rule.[6] Under

125

the legendary Dagestani chieftain, Shamil, the areas that today form southern Chechnya and inner Dagestan formed a shrinking independent Islamic state, an Imamate, from 1824 until the Russian capture of Shamil in 1859.[7] The Circassian rebels were not defeated until the mass expulsion of Circassians to the Ottoman Empire in 1864.

Even following the incorporation of the North Caucasus into the Russian empire, the northeastern regions were only partially pacified, but never appeared to become integrated with Russia in ways that other minority-dominated areas, such as in the Volga region, did. The physical expulsion of the majority of the Circassian population helped Russia manage the northwestern Caucasus; but Chechnya and Dagestan remained unruly. Whenever Russia was at war or otherwise weakened, these lands saw rebellions of varying length and strength. This occurred after World War I during the Russian civil war 1918-21, and, though in a much smaller scale, during the collectivization of the 1930s and World War II. In 1944, this obstinate refusal to submit had tragic consequences. Falsely claiming that Chechens, Ingush, Karachai, and Balkars had collaborated with the invading German forces, Joseph Stalin in February 1944 ordered the wholesale deportation of these peoples to Central Asia. Entire populations were loaded on cattle wagons and transported in the middle of winter to the steppes of Central Asia, where little preparation had been made for their arrival. An estimated quarter of the deportees died during transport or shortly after arrival due to cold, hunger, or epidemics.[8]

The largest number of the deported peoples of the North Caucasus was the Chechens. However, until deportation, Chechens primarily identified with their

Teip or clan, not as members of a Chechen nation. More than anything, deportation helped develop national consciousness among the Chechens. The demographic consequences of deportation and the 13-year exile of the Chechens until they were allowed to return in 1957 are very tangible. Between 1926-37, the Chechen population increased by 36 percent; in another 11-year period, between 1959 and 1970, the figure was 46 percent. But during the 20-year period from 1939-59, the rate of increase was only 2.5 percent, although the population would almost have doubled under normal circumstances.[9] Thus, it is difficult to overstate the importance of the deportations in the collective memory of the punished peoples. With regard to the Chechens, it had important political consequences that did not immediately materialize among the much smaller Ingush, Karachai, and Balkar populations. Most leaders of the Chechen movement for independence in the 1990s were either born or grew up in exile in Kazakhstan. The deportation convinced many Chechens that there was no way for them to live securely under Russian rule; it also explains the extent of support for separation from Russia among the people and perhaps the readiness among portions of the population to embrace radical ideologies of resistance.

After the August coup in Moscow against Mikhail Gorbachev that spelled the end of the Soviet Union, most constituent republics declared their independence. So did two autonomous republics within the Russian Federation: Chechnya and Tatarstan. Tatarstan, encircled by Russia proper, began negotiations on mutual relations with Moscow that eventually led to a deal in 1994 that granted Tatarstan broad autonomy. In Chechnya, however, the nationalist movement in power was less compromising. General Jokhar Dudayev, who had seized power from the former communist leadership in September 1991, was elected President of Chechnya and declared its independence soon after. Chechnya, in this context, stood out by being the only autonomous republic in Russia where a nationalist movement took power and ousted the communist party leadership. In this sense, it resembled the developments in Georgia and Armenia more than that of the Central Asian republics or Russia's other autonomous republics: The leadership consisted of true nationalists, not former Communist elites that cloaked a nationalist mantle.

While Russian President Boris Yeltsin made an abortive attempt to rein in Dudayev by sending special forces to Chechnya to restore Moscow's rule, Dudayev had managed to create a presidential guard that was enough of a deterrent to avoid Russian military action. At this point, Russia was itself in a chaotic situation. Yeltsin was preoccupied with building Russian statehood, and Chechnya was put on the back burner. However, by 1994, Yeltsin had consolidated his power after physically attacking his parliamentary opposition in October 1993 — an action that indebted him to the military and security forces. Chechnya hence remained as a thorn in the eye of a rising Russia. Moreover, Chechnya's de facto independence and the heavily anti-Russian rhetoric emanating from Dudayev was foiling Russian plans of asserting control over the South Caucasus states of Azerbaijan and Georgia, in particular controlling the westward export of Caspian oil resources. Thus, for both internal and external reasons, the Russian government was now prompted to "solve" the Chechnya problem. Serious negotiations between Moscow and Grozny were never attempted, mainly because of the personal enmity between Dudayev and Yeltsin.[10] After seeking briefly to use subversion to overthrow Dudayev without success, the Russian government decided to launch a wholesale invasion of Chechnya in late 1994.[11]

Importantly, the Chechen movement for independence was an almost entirely secular affair.[12] Its chief leaders, such as Jokhar Dudayev and Aslan Maskhadov, were former Soviet officers with highly secular lifestyles. This is not to say that Islamist elements were not present: They did develop among the Chechen leadership, mainly through the efforts of Zelimkhan Yandarbiyev and Movladi Udugov, high officials in Dudayev's administration. However, they remained largely marginal, being able to assert themselves only tepidly during the internal crisis that Dudayev experienced in 1993, in which he briefly began using increasingly religious language in an attempt to shore up legitimacy when faced with growing criticism of his mismanagement of Chechnya's economy. Moreover, there is significant evidence suggesting that Yandarbiyev and Uduguov embraced Islamism in a mainly instrumental way.[13]

The First War.

Contrary to Moscow's expectations, the Russian threat rallied erstwhile skeptics around Dudayev once the war started. Aided by the dismal character of the Russian military campaign, the Chechen forces were able to resist the Russian invasion. Getting bogged down in Chechnya, the Russian military resorted to brutal tactics to subdue an opponent they had thoroughly underestimated, and used air bombing and artillery to level Grozny before entering it. Only after 2 months did the Russian army manage to estab-

129

lish control over the city—at the cost of thousands of Russian casualties, over 20,000 killed civilians, a total destruction of the city, and hundreds of thousands of refugees. The war continued, with the Chechen forces regrouping in the south of Chechnya. Meanwhile, Dudayev himself was killed by Russian forces in April 1996. Despite this setback, the Chechen forces in August 1996 managed to stage a counteroffensive, and retake the three major cities of Chechnya, including Grozny, in 3 days of fighting. This amounted to a total humiliation of the Russian forces, and the government was forced to end the war and pull out all its forces by a cease-fire signed 3 weeks later.

The war led to the total devastation of Grozny and many other Chechen towns and villages. According to the most credible estimates, the death toll in the first war was in the range of 50,000 people.[14] Compared with the war in Afghanistan, the Chechen war was far more lethal for the Russian army. During 1984, the worst year in Afghanistan, almost 2,500 Soviet soldiers were killed. In Chechnya, Russian losses surpassed this number within 4 months of the intervention. At its highest, the shelling of Grozny, counted by the number of explosions per day, surpassed the shelling of Sarajevo in the early 1990s by a factor of at least 50. Grozny was literally leveled to the ground in a destruction that recalled the battle of Stalingrad.

Moreover, the war was dominated by massive human rights violations, which are considered the worst in Europe since World War II. Russian forces engaged in several well-documented massacres of civilians, the most well-known of which occurred in the village of Samashki in April 1995. As noted above, the first war in Chechnya was waged almost exclusively in the name of national independence. But it is in the context of the brutality of the Russian onslaught that the first jihadi elements appeared in Chechnya. Indeed, it is also the context in which the Chechen leadership and fighters welcomed or tolerated these foreign recruits; there is ample evidence that there was little love lost between the Chechen leadership and the jihadis—but the Chechens needed all the help that they could get, and were hardly in a position to turn away these new-found allies, all the more since they were exceptionally effective in combat.

Similarly, this is the context in which terrorist tactics enter the Chechen war. Practiced from the outset by the Russian detachments, some of the Chechens commanders gradually came to employ them. Here, the notorious Shamil Basayev deserves particular mention, whose hostage-taking raid on a hospital in the southern Russian town of Budyonnovsk in June 1995 was the first large-scale use of terrorism by the Chechens. It occurred at a time when the Chechen cause seemed all but lost, and arguably contributed to turning the tide in the war, or at least in forestalling defeat. Basayev himself was in one sense an unlikely terrorist: Only 3 years earlier, he had deployed as a volunteer to fight the Georgians in Abkhazia, being among the North Caucasian volunteers that received training and assistance for the purpose from the Russian military intelligence services.[15]

The number of foreign fighters in the first war was small, perhaps a few hundred at most. These were mainly the roving "Arab Afghans" who had fought in Kashmir, Tajikistan, and Bosnia-Herzegovina, which was the big focus of jihadi attention in the early 1990s. Tellingly, the person who actually declared a jihad on Russia was none other than Akhmad Kadyrov, then mufti of Chechnya, who would switch sides in 1999, and became Russia's local satrap, a position his son, Ramzan, inherited upon his assassination in May 2004.

The Inter-War Period.

The August 1996 accords, complemented by a formal peace treaty in May 1997, granted Chechnya de facto independence, though the issue of Chechnya's status was deferred until December 31, 2001. In practice, Chechnya had the opportunity to build what in practice amounted to an independent state. Russian law did not apply in Chechnya, and no Russian police, army, customs, or postal service operated there.

However, for both internal and external reasons, this second attempt at independence in a decade ended in a dismal failure. Russia consistently prevented Chechnya from seeking outside financial help, and though it committed funds to the reconstruction of the war-ravaged republic, $100 million disappeared before they even reached Chechnya. In a celebrated statement, President Yeltsin publicly admitted "only the devil" knew where the money had gone.[16] Hence the basis on which the Chechen government could create a functioning state was shaky indeed.

Yet initial signals were positive. In a presidential election that the Organization for Security and Cooperation in Europe (OSCE) termed largely free and fair, the population of Chechnya overwhelmingly voted for Aslan Maskhadov, Chief of Staff of the Chechen armed forces and the most moderate among the three presidential contenders. Thus, Chechnya acquired a legitimate government that was open to compromise and cooperation, although it never wavered from its commitment to an independent Chechnya. Sadly, this initial stability did not last. Chechnya was awash with young, unemployed war veterans with arsenals of weapons, whose loyalty was to individual field commanders rather than to the central Chechen government. With the economic depression deepening, Maskhadov's authority over Chechnya gradually diminished, and the government became unable to uphold law and order. Various criminal groups emerged that engaged in smuggling and kidnapping, and the government showed its inability to effectively deal with this problem. Most alarmingly, warlords Shamil Basayev and the Jordanian-born Khattab began planning for the unification of Chechnya with the neighboring republic of Dagestan, still part of the Russian Federation. Maskhadov was either unwilling or unable to rein in these warlords, fearing an intra-Chechen war. As a result, Basayev and Khattab were able to recruit hundreds of Dagestanis and other North Caucasians, including Chechens, into what they termed an Islamic Brigade based in Southeastern Chechnya. This brigade would eventually launch the incursion into Dagestan in August 1999, which precipitated the second war.

It is instructive, at this point, to compare Chechnya to the major other armed conflict in Europe of the time: Bosnia-Herzegovina. In fact, Chechnya was similar to Bosnia in terms of the level and character of the jihadi presence; where it differed was in the absence of a Dayton-type internationalized conflict management mechanism.

Indeed, most jihadis that came to fight in Chechnya were veterans of the Bosnian campaign. This was true for the poster child of Chechen jihadis, the Saudi-born Amir al-Khattab. What is seldom recalled is the extent of the Islamist contagion in Bosnia at the time of the Dayton Accords. Indeed, the leadership of the

Bosnian Muslims in many ways leaned more toward Islamism than that of the Chechens: Alija Izetbegovic, the Bosnian Muslim leader, had a long history of Islamist inclinations dating back to his involvement in the Young Muslim organizations in Bosnia, *Mladi Muslimani*, during World War II .[17] Haris Silajdzic, his closest advisor, received Islamic education in Libya and served as an advisor to Bosnia's spiritual leader, the *Reis-ul-Ulema*. By contrast, the only Islamist to lead the Chechen resistance was Yandarbiyev, who only served as interim president between Dudayev's death in April 1996 and Maskhadov's election in January 1997. By contrast, Dudayev and Maskhadov were considerably more secular than the key Bosnian leaders.

The jihadi presence in Bosnia was a real problem at the close of the war. The Bosnian leadership was split between those wanting to rid Bosnia of the foreign radicals, and those grateful for their support and who wanted to allow them to stay. Most jihadis were nevertheless evicted shortly following the Dayton Accords, after several altercations with North Atlantic Treaty Organization (NATO) forces brought attention to their presence.[18] Indeed, this highlights the main difference between Bosnia and Chechnya: Chechnya had the Khasavyurt treaty that postponed the key issue in the conflict; was never fully implemented; was bilateral and lacked any international guarantor; and lacked international peacekeeping forces. Bosnia, on the other hand, had a real peace treaty, and NATO forces to keep that treaty. Thus, most jihadis were gradually evicted from Bosnia following the Dayton Accords. However, small numbers remained until as late as 2007, when the Bosnian government finally removed the last remnants.[19]

In Chechnya, there was no force capable of removing the jihadi elements. Indeed, the Maskhadov administration was considerably weaker than its Bosnian counterpart, and could not rely on an international force, whether military such as the NATO Implementation Forces (IFOR) or civilian such as the Office of the High Representative. Unlike Bosnia, which was awash in international assistance already a year following the Dayton Accords, Chechnya received next to no foreign assistance. Thus, the crippled Maskhadov government was in no position to successfully oust the jihadis. This was not for a lack of trying: In 1998, there was even fire exchanged between the Chechen government forces and jihadi groups. But unlike in Bosnia, the jihadi forces led by Khattab had found a powerful local ally in Shamil Basayev. Maskhadov was thus faced with a dire choice. He could either confront the jihadis that had ensconced themselves in southeastern Chechnya, at the cost of a Chechen civil war; or he could tolerate their presence, preserving peace and trying to strengthen state institutions. In the end, he chose the latter—which appeared the lesser of two evils. While he even sought a deal with Moscow in rooting out the radicals, a call that went unanswered, his decision contributed greatly to the failure of Chechen state-building and led directly to the second war.[20]

Thus, the Chechnya-based jihadis coalesced with Wahhabi groups that had emerged independently in Dagestan in the late 1990s. Training camps developed modeled on those in Afghanistan, where small numbers of people from the entire North Caucasus and beyond received training; many then fought in the second Chechen war, and subsequently spread the militant ideology and tactics back to their own home republics.

The Second War.

During the course of the second Chechen war, which began in October 1999, concern grew over the radicalization of the Chechen resistance movement and its links to extremist Islamic groups in the Middle East. Indeed, authors like Gordon Hahn have come to conclude that the "key, if not main factor driving the violence in the North Caucasus" is "the salience of local cultural and the Salafist jihadist theo-ideology and the influence of the global jihadi revolutionary movement."[21] While this chapter takes issue with that claim, the Chechen resistance has indeed acquired a much stronger Islamic character. The use of Islamic vocabulary such as jihad (holy war) or mujahedin (resistance fighters) increased markedly, as did active support for the Chechen cause by radical Islamic groups in the Middle East, at least until the U.S. invasion of Iraq led jihadis to flock to that conflict.

Moscow managed to drive this point across especially after September 11, 2001 (9/11). Immediately after the terrorist attacks on the United States, the Russian leadership began drawing comparisons between the attacks and the situation in Chechnya. Only hours after the collapse of the World Trade Centers, Russian State television broadcast a statement by President Vladimir Putin expressing solidarity with the American people, but also reminding the audience of Russia's earlier warnings of the common threat of "Islamic Fundamentalism." This marked the beginning of a strategy aiming to capitalize on the tragic attacks on America by highlighting the alleged parallels between the attacks on the United States and the situation in Chechnya. "The Russian people understand the American people better than anyone else, having experienced terrorism first-hand," President Putin said the day after the attacks.[22]

This turned out to be the harbinger of a diplomatic campaign targeted at Western countries intended to shore up legitimacy, if not support, for the Russian army's violent crackdown in Chechnya.[23] This campaign was part and parcel of a five-step strategy to reduce the negative fallout of the war in Chechnya. The first component of that strategy was to isolate the conflict zone and prevent both Russian and international media from reporting on the conflict independently. The kidnapping of Andrei Babitsky, a reporter for Radio Liberty, early on served as a warning for journalists of the consequences of ignoring Moscow's rules on reporting the conflict. Since then, only a few journalists have actually been able to provide independent reporting from Chechnya. Most prominent has been the late Russian journalist, Anna Politkovskaya who was murdered in Moscow in 2007, and French writer, Anne Nivat.

The second prong in the strategy was to rename the conflict: Instead of a "war," it was an "anti-terrorist operation." Third, and stemming directly from this, Russia sought to discredit the Chechen struggle and undermine its leadership by accusing them individually and collectively of involvement with terrorism. Russia's campaign against Chechen President Aslan Maskhadov's chief negotiator, Akhmed Zakayev, is one example of this. This nevertheless backfired as first Denmark and then Great Britain refused to extradite Zakayev to Russia; Great Britain instead providing him with political asylum. Fourth, Russia sought to "Chechenize" the conflict and turn it into an intra-Chechen confrontation by setting up and arming a brutal but ethnically Chechen puppet regime in Grozny under Kadyrov, the former Mufti (a professional jurist interpreting Muslin law) of the republic. This would reduce Russian casualties and enable hostilities to be depicted as a war between Chechen factions that Russia was helping to stabilize. Fifth, after branding the war as an anti-terrorist campaign, discrediting the rebel leadership, and trying to turn the war into a civil war among Chechens, Russia declared that the war was over.

The second war proved as heavy on the civilian population as the first. In many ways, Russian abuses were more systematic. For example, the Russian leadership set up what they termed "filtration camps" — essentially concentration camps that gathered male Chechens of fighting age, and in which torture and disappearances were rampant.[24] Whereas European countries and the United States kept a moderate but noticeable level of criticism against Russia's massive human rights violations in Chechnya during both the first war in 1994-96 and in 1999-2001, Russia succeeded in convincing western observers it was not fighting a people, but terrorists. In an atmosphere of increased cooperation between Russia and the West, with American need for Russian intelligence and cooperation in Afghanistan, a halt to criticism on Chechnya became the foremost price Russia managed to extract.

A Regional Insurgency.

Today, the nationalist Chechen leadership is almost exclusively an expatriate phenomenon. The Chechen Republic of Ichkeria has for all practical purposes ceased to exist; instead, the insurgency brands itself the "Caucasus Emirate" (CE), overtly boasts of its belonging to the global jihad, and operates across the North Caucasus. Studies of violent incidents in the North Caucasus agree that the violence peaked in April 2001, 18 months into the second Chechen war. From 2002 to 2006, violence was fairly steady before declining to a low point in 2006-07.[25] From 2007 onwards, however, violence has been on a steady increase, albeit fluctuating in both intensity and regional focus. Already in 2005, Dagestan and Ingushetia began seeing escalating violence, rivaling at times the levels in Chechnya.[26] Since 2007, the situation has continued to deteriorate, with the number of violent incidents rising sharply every year from 2007 to 2010.[27] In 2009 alone, for example, the number of violent incidents went from 795 to 1,100, with fatalities mounting from 586 to 900.[28] In the first 11 months of 2010, federal prosecutors acknowledged the death of 218 security personnel and the wounding of 536.[29] From 2008 onward, Dagestan and Ingushetia have alternated in the lead in the frequency of incidents.[30] In 2010 and 2011, the violence escalated significantly in the Western republic of KBR as well—marking the diffusion of large-scale and enduring violence beyond the republics bordering Chechnya. Thus, in 2010 political violence claimed 79 deaths and 39 wounded; the first 11 months of 2011 saw those figures rise to 98 and 39, respectively.[31] As if this was not enough, 2011 also saw violence spread to North Ossetia, a traditionally calm and majority Orthodox Christian republic.[32]

RUSSIAN POLICIES

What role did Russian policies play in transforming the conflict from a contained, nationalist rebellion to a sprawling jihadi insurgency? Counterintuitively as it may seem, Russian policies have contributed directly to this development. In another parallel to the Bosnian conflict, Russian rhetoric mirrored that of the Serbs: misunderstood defenders of Europe against the threat of Islamic radicalism, the "green wave." Indeed, this line of reasoning has been visible in Russian outreach efforts since the mid-1990s, with increasing fervor following 9/11.[33] But more than just arguing for their case, Russian officials actively worked to make the reality of the conflict conform to their vision of it. Thus, there was a remarkable pattern in Russia's priorities during the second war: the priority given to targeting the nationalist Chechen leadership rather than the jihadi elements within it. Therefore, on the battlefield, Russia targeted field commanders like Ruslan Gelayev, as well as Maskhadov himself, whom Russian forces killed in March 2005. On the diplomatic front, Russian diplomats and lawyers furiously prosecuted and sought the extradition of secular leaders like Zakayev and Maskhadov's foreign minister, Ilyas Akhmadov. By comparison, Islamist Chechen leaders have fared much better. Among exiles, Movladi Udugov remains alive, among the few remaining members of the first generation of Chechen leaders to survive. Yandarbiyev was killed in Qatar by Russian agents, but only in 2004. Similarly, the current leader of the CE, Dokka Umarov, has served since June 2006. The most notorious Chechen warlord, Shamil Basayev, was killed in 2006, but not necessarily by the Russians. French journalist, Anne Nivat, once wrote that the safest place in Chechnya was near Shamil Basayev: Russian bombs never appeared to fall there. Given Basayev's connection with Russian special forces (GRU) through the conflict in Abkhazia, numerous conspiracy theories emerged of Basayev's continued relationship with Russian state institutions; indeed, news reports following his death suggested that he was killed accidently by explosives in the truck he was driving in mountain roads in Ingushetia.[34]

While allegations of Basayev's GRU connections during the Georgia-Abkhaz war are well-established,[35] those concerning subsequent periods are based mainly on innuendo. Clearer evidence is available in the case of Arbi Barayev, one of the most viciously militant as well as most criminalized of Chechnya's warlords. Barayev was one of the key forces seeking to undermine Maskhadov's leadership in the interwar era; it was his group that kidnapped and beheaded foreign telecommunications workers in 1998, effectively forcing out the small international presence in Chechnya. Similarly, it was Barayev's forces that engaged in firefights with Maskhadov's troops in 1998. Following the renewed warfare, Barayev lived freely in the town of Alkhan-Kala, under Russian control, until his death in 2001—despite the fact that he was responsible for gruesome, video-recorded murders of captive Russian servicemen. As several observers have noted, his opulent residence was only a few miles away from a Russian checkpoint near his native Alkhan-Kala, while his car had an FSB identification which allowed him to race through Russian checkpoints.[36] Tellingly, Barayev was killed by a GRU hit squad only after the FSB's then-head of counterterrorism, General Ugryumov, had died. The apparent conclusion was that Ugryumov provided a cover for Barayev, and the former's death made it possible for the GRU to take Barayev out.

Given the nature of this conflict, evidence can at best be inconclusive. But circumstantial evidence suggests two things: First, that during the second war there was no clear and unified chain of command on either the Chechen or the Russian side. Chechen forces paid nominal allegiance to Maskhadov but, in practice, field commanders behaved independently, and with little coordination. On the Russian side, detachments of the army, GRU, FSB, and Ministry of Interior played different roles in the conflict, roles that were poorly coordinated; moreover, they each appeared to keep ties with some Chechen commanders, while combating others. Second, the policies of the Russian leadership itself contributed to change the nature of the conflict from a nationalist rebellion to one where the enemy was Islamic jihadis. While this is likely in the long run to be of greater danger to Russia, it did succeed in making the conflict fit into Moscow's desired narrative. After all, Maskhadov and the Chechen nationalist leadership was respected in Western circles, being granted meetings with Western officials and maintaining strong support among Western media, civil society, and human rights organizations. The jihadi elements, needless to say, did not and do not enjoy this status.

In a sense, however, Moscow is now faced both with a jihadi movement *and* a nationalist Chechnya. Indeed, the CE is everything it is blamed of being: a part of the global jihad, and a terrorist incubator on Europe's borders. While primarily led by Chechens, it is most active in the other republics of the North Caucasus. But Moscow also is faced with a nationalist Chechen leadership in Grozny. Indeed, the Kadyrov administration appointed by Moscow has developed in such a nationalistic direction that the secular Chechen nationalists in exile, who broke with the Islamist faction with the establishment of the Emirate in 2007, began mending fences with Kadyrov, their erstwhile foe, by 2009.[37] While a counterintuitive turn, the secular nationalists concluded that Kadyrov has in practice achieved what they failed to achieve through an armed rebellion: a Chechen republic that is for most practical purposes behaving as an independent entity. As early as 2005, Russian analysts began referring to Kadyrov's moves as "separatism-light."[38]

A PACIFIED CHECHNYA?

Presently, Chechnya is arguably among the least violence-ridden republics in the North Caucasus. The last several years have seen widespread violence in Dagestan, Ingushetia, and KBR; by comparison, Chechnya has been relatively stable. But the long-term outlook is clouded by the fragility on which this relative quiet rests.

The main reason for Chechnya's stability is the dominance that Ramzan Kadyrov and his militia forces exert over the republic. These fighters, estimated at over 5,000 in number, consist mainly of former resistance fighters. Moscow initially sought to balance the Kadyrov clan with other political figures. Following Akhmad Kadyrov's assassination, Ramzan—who had not yet achieved the eligible age for the presidency—was appointed deputy prime minister. Chechnya was instead led by career police officer Alu Alkhanov, who had sided with Moscow already in the first war. By March 2006, Ramzan Kadyrov was elevated to the post of Prime Minister, replacing Sergey Abramov. Less than a year later, Alkhanov was dismissed and Kadyrov appointed President. Thus, by 2007, any political balances to Kadyrov had been removed; fighting forces outside his control nevertheless remained: the "Zapad" and "Vostok" battalions, the latter commanded by Sulim Yamadayev, were nevertheless disbanded in November 2008 following escalating tensions and actual armed clashes with Kadyrov's forces. Yamadayev loyalists were evicted from Chechnya; Sulim Yamadayev was assassinated in Dubai in 2009, while his brother met the same fate in Moscow, presumably at Kadyrov's orders.[39] This removed the sole remaining check on Kadyrov's power in Chechnya, to the chagrin of many decisionmakers in Moscow—but with the apparent blessing of Putin and Kadyrov's immediate handler, the Chechen-born Vladislav Surkov, who serves as Putin's first deputy chief of staff and chief ideologue.

Kadyrov has walked a fine line between vows of absolute personal loyalty and subservience to Vladimir Putin, on the one hand, and institutional distancing from Russia. Thus, in 2007, he repeatedly urged Putin to stay on as president for life.[40] In 2009, Kadyrov said "if it was not for Putin, Chechnya would not exist."[41] In January 2010, he added that "I am completely Vladimir Putin's man. I would rather die 100 times than let him down."[42] Kadyrov also delivers votes for the ruling party. In 2007, for example, official figures showed that 99.5 percent of the Chechen electorate cast their votes, and that 99.3 percent voted for the United Russia party.

On the other hand, Kadyrov has increasingly appealed to Chechen nationalism and sought to Islamize Chechnya. In December 2006, he publicly sought the prosecution of Russian officers responsible for civilian deaths in Chechnya.[43] His attitude toward the Russian military, which he sought to have expelled from Chechnya, is best illustrated by his 2006 statement that "as for the generals, I'm not going to say that I care about their opinion."[44] Following his appointment as President, Kadyrov moved strongly to assert

Chechnya's economic and political autonomy. For example, he has sought the creation of a Chechen oil company that would keep the revenues of Chechnya's oil industry instead of sending them to Moscow; and campaigned to have Chechens convicted elsewhere in Russia serve prison time in Chechnya.[45] Already in 2006, Kadyrov began urging women to comply with Islamic dress codes, something that was later officially promulgated with a program to strengthen "female virtue."[46] He has also spoken favorably of Shariah in general, and of both honor killings and of polygamy in particular, and referred to women as men's property—all of which are in violation of Russian laws.[47]

Adding to this, Kadyrov has made a habit of diverting the enormous funds coming to Chechnya from the federal center. Indeed, Russian state auditors have repeatedly noted the disappearance of the equivalent of dozens of millions of dollars in state subsidies to Chechnya, which amount to 90 percent of the republic's budget.

Thus, all in all, Kadyrov has stabilized Chechnya on the surface. But the stability rests on a very weak foundation. On the one hand, it rests solely on the personal relationship between Kadyrov and Putin. As such, the question is whether the stability of the republic would outlive the departure from power of either man. Given the average life expectancy of Chechen politicians, the possibility of Kadyrov being assassinated is very real. If that were to happen, would the thousands of former rebels now forming the bulk of his militia pledge loyalty to a new leader, or would they return to the resistance, ushering in a third Chechen war? Even if Kadyrov remains in power, the defection of large sections of his militia to the resistance cannot be excluded. Similarly, Kadyrov's pragmatism is exhibited by his decision to switch sides from the resistance to Russia. It is not inconceivable that he could switch sides again under some scenario—for example, if Putin were to leave power and his successor would discontinue the arrangement with Kadyrov. Before her death, Anna Politkovskaya observed that by his policies in Chechnya, Putin had essentially guaranteed a third Chechen war at some future point. She may have turned out to be prescient.[48]

CONCLUSION

The North Caucasus is sinking ever deeper into a process of Afghanization. While the external impetus of jihadi ideology has played a role in this development, this chapter has sought to show that the root cause of the region's decline is the Russian government's policies—in particular its prosecution of the wars in Chechnya; its over-reliance on repression in both Chechnya and the rest of the region; its centralization of power; its unwillingness to allow the North Caucasus to open up to the rest of the world; its failure to provide an economic future for the region's population; a political discourse that is making North Caucasians increasingly estranged from Russian society; and the corruption and criminalization of the Russian political system.

This situation destabilizes Russia, and forms its most acute political problem. But it does not only affect Russia: It greatly affects the security and prosperity of the South Caucasus, as well as potentially all of Europe. The impact on the South Caucasus is threefold. Most obviously, Azerbaijan and Georgia are directly affected by the violence and economic woes of the region. This is only likely to be exacerbated in the future: While Azerbaijan experiences rapid growth thanks to its oil and gas industry, Georgia has made great strides in reforms, not least in terms of practically abolishing administrative corruption. Over time, the contrast between these economies and the languishing North Caucasus will have consequences, in terms, for example, of migration flows. Secondly, the southern neighbors of the North Caucasus are affected by the diffusion of the conflicts in the North. Thus, flows of refugees—and fighters—from the North Caucasus into Georgia and Azerbaijan have been a recurring phenomenon over the past 2 decades, with destabilizing effects on both countries. Third, the Russian government has shown a distinctive tendency to assign blame to its neighbors when it has proven unable to deal with the consequences of its own failures in the North Caucasus. In the beginning of the second Chechnyan war, both Azerbaijan and Georgia were accused, without a shred of evidence, of serving as conduits for thousands of foreign fighters to Chechnya; ever since, Russian accusations have focused on Georgia, with threats of intervention into the Pankisi Gorge on Georgian territory in 2002, and actual instances of Russian bombings of the Gorge.[49] Following the escalation of violence in 2008-11, Russian officials have made a custom of blaming Georgia—and occasionally Western powers—for actively colluding with the jihadi rebels in the North Caucasus. Thus, Russia's tendency to blame others for its failures poses a constant risk to its neighbors.

This predicament is most acute, given the upcoming Olympic Games in Sochi. Given current trends, Moscow is unlikely to be able to pacify the North Caucasus ahead of the Games, and will be increasingly likely to blame others for any terrorist attacks that would threaten this prestigious event. The alternative option, a gigantic security operation to assert control over the region, would itself very likely have a spill-over effect on the South Caucasus.

Beyond the Caucasus itself, Russia's misrule in the North Caucasus poses a threat to Europe as a whole. In fact, with the European Union (EU) now extended to the shores of the Black Sea, it is a direct neighbor of the North Caucasus. Through the Eastern Partnership, Partnership for Peace, and other instruments, the EU and NATO are seeking to contribute to the building of stability, security, and prosperity in their eastern neighborhood. In spite of the unresolved conflicts of the South Caucasus and Moldova, and the mixed scorecard for democratic development across the region, the Eastern neighborhood has indeed seen largely positive trends over the past decade. But the North Caucasus is the sole remaining area where Europe has little to no ability to influence developments, but which could nevertheless have a considerably negative effect on Europe. The region is already a trans-shipment point for smuggled goods to Europe, and an incubator of jihadi elements from the region and beyond. Thus far, the Islamic Emirate has stayed focused on targets in the North Caucasus and Russia. But given its broader ideological orientation and its perception of Europe as a collaborator with Russia in the repression of Muslims, the prospect of groups affiliated with the Emirate targeting Europe itself should not be excluded. After all, jihadi elements with connections to Central Asia have already been implicated in planned terrorist attacks in Germany and elsewhere in Europe.

Thus, Russia's failure to stabilize the North Caucasus has amounted to the creation of an Afghanistan-like environment in Europe: a failed state within a state. Moscow is patently unable to remedy the situation, seeming only to design policies that are as a whole counterproductive. Unfortunately, the failure of Russia to address the region's problems is related directly to Russia's very system. The sad fact is that as long as Russia itself maintains a political system based on kleptocratic authoritarianism, the prospects of the North Caucasus will remain dim.

This poses a conundrum for Western powers. If the situation continues to deteriorate, Western powers may not be able to afford simply treating the North Caucasus as a domestic Russian issue. At the same time, their policy options in designing responses to the situation in the region are highly limited. While efforts could be undertake in conjunction with the South Caucasian states to contain the destabilization emanating from the North Caucasus, addressing the root causes of the problem will require a dialogue with Moscow, the prospects of which are dim.

ENDNOTES - CHAPTER 3

1. Marina Kamenev, "Has Russia Lost Control of the North Caucasus?" *Time*, June 12, 2009, available from *www.time.com/time/world/article/0,8599,1904234,00.html*; Emil Souleimonov, "Dagestan: the Emerging Core of the North Caucasus Insurgency," *Central Asia-Caucasus Analyst*, September 29, 2010, available from *www.cacianalyst.org/?q=node/5415*.

2. Olof Staaf, "Moscow Unable to Afford New Development Program for the North Caucasus," *Central Asia-Caucasus Analyst*, August 17, 2011, available from *www.cacianalyst.org/?q=node/5614*; "Moscow Hosts Rally under the Motto 'Stop Feeding Caucasus!'" *Caucasian Knot*, October 22, 2011, available from *rf.eng.kavkaz-uzel.ru/articles/18748*.

3. Charles Blandy, *North Caucasus: On the Brink of Far-Reaching Destabilisation*, Caucasus Series, 05/36, Shrivenham, UK: United

Kingdom Defence Academy, Conflict Studies Research Center, August 2005, p. 6.

4. Sergey Markedonov, "'Russkiy Vopros' v kavkazskom izmerenii" ("The 'Russian question' in the Caucasian dimension"), *Caucasus Times*, April 9, 2007, available from *www.caucasustimes.com/article.asp?id=12365*; Olga I. Vendina *et al.*, "The Wars in Chechnya and their Effects on Neighboring Regions," *Eurasian Geography and Economics*, Vol. 48, No. 2, 2007, pp. 194-195, available from *www.colorado.edu/ibs/waroutcomes/docs/EGE_2007_WarChechnya_s4.pdf*.

5. Paul Goble, "Kabardino-Balkaria Highlights Putin's 'Failure' in the Caucasus," *Window on Eurasia*, January 23, 2008, available from *windowoneurasia.blogspot.com/2008/01/window-on-eurasia-kabardino-balkaria.html*.

6. Marie Bennigsen Broxup, ed., *The North Caucasus Barrier*, London, UK: C. Hurst, 1992; John Dunlop, *Russia Confronts Chechnya: Roots of a Separatist Conflict*, Cambridge, UK: Cambridge University Press, 1998, pp. 1-40.

7. Moshe Gammer, *Muslim Resistance to the Tsar: Shamil and the Conquest of Chechnia and Daghestan*, London, UK: Routledge, 2003.

8. Aleksandr Nekrich, *The Punished Peoples: The Deportation and Fate of Soviet Minorities at the End of the Second World War*, New York: W.W. Norton, 1981; Carlotta Gall and Thomas de Waal, *Chechnya: A Small Victorious War*, Basingstoke, UK: Pan Books, 1997, pp. 56-75.

9. Robert Conquest, *The Nation Killers: The Soviet Deportation of Nationalities*, London, UK: MacMillan, 1970, p. 160.

10. See Gall and de Waal, *Chechnya: A Small Victorious War*.

11. For details, see Chap. 5, "The War in Chechnya," in Svante E. Cornell, *Small Nations and Great Powers: A Study of Ethnopolitical Conflict in the Caucasus*, Richmond, VA: Curzon Press, 2001.

12. Emil Souleimanov, "Chechnya, Wahhabism and the Invasion of Dagestan," *Middle East Review of International Affairs*, Vol. 9, No. 4, December 2005, pp. 48-71.

13. Julie Wilhelmsen, "Between a Rock and a Hard Place: The Islamisation of the Chechen Separatist Movement," *Europe-Asia Studies*, Vol. 57, No. 1, January 2005, pp. 38-39.

14. John B. Dunlop, "How Many Soldiers and Civilians Died During the Russo-Chechen War of 1994-96?" *Central Asian Survey*, Vol. 19, No. 3/4, 2000, pp. 328-338.

15. Boris Kagarlitsky, *Russia under Yeltsin and Putin: Neo-Liberal Autocracy*, London, UK: Pluto Press, 2002, pp. 229-234. Russian press reports in *Novaya Gazeta, Rossiyskaya Gazeta, and Versiya* have all provided documentation to this effect.

16. Peter Ford, "Yeltsin Admits Aid Misses Chechnya," *Christian Science Monitor*, August 19, 1997. Only $21 million of the $138 million committed eventually reached Chechnya.

17. Gerard F. Powers, "Religion, Conflict and Prospects for Peace in Bosnia, Croatia, and Yugoslavia," *Journal of International Affairs*, Vol. 50, No. 1, Summer 1996, available from *www.georgefox. edu/academics/undergrad/departments/soc-swk/ree/Powers_Religion_ Oct%201996.pdf*.

18. See Evan Kohlmann, *Al Qaeda's Jihad in Europe: The Afghan-Bosnian Network*, Oxford, UK: Berg Publications, 2004; Michael A. Innes, *Denial of Sanctuary: Understanding Terrorist Safe Havens*, Westport, CT: Praeger, 1997, pp. 55-56.

19. Anes Alic, "Foreign jihadis face Deportation in Bosnia-Herzegovina," *Jamestown Terrorism Monitor*, Vol. 5, No. 21, 8 November 2007, available from *www.jamestown.org/ programs/gta/single/?tx_ttnews%5Btt_news%5D=4532&tx_ ttnews%5BbackPid%5D=182&no_cache=1*.

20. See Wilhelmsen, "Between a Rock and a Hard Place," pp. 46-50.

21. Gordon M. Hahn, *Getting the Caucasus Emirate Right*, Washington, DC: Center for Strategic and International Studies, August 2011, p. 1.

22. RTR (Russian State Television), September 12, 2001, 1300 GMT. See also Francesca Mereu, "U.S.: Russia Says Chechen Conflict Aids 'Understanding' Of U.S. Tragedy," RFE/RL, September 14, 2001.

23. See Janusz Bugajski, "Beware of Putin Bearing Gifts," *The Washington Times*, October 10, 2001.

24. Human Rights Watch, "Hundreds of Chechens Detained in 'Filtration Camps'," February 17, 2000, available from *www.hrw. org/news/2000/02/17/hundreds-chechens-detained-filtration-camps*.

25. John O'Loughlin and Frank D. W. Witmer, "The Localized Geographies of Violence in the North Caucasus of Russia," *Annals of the Association of American Geographers*, Vol. 101, No. 1, 2011, pp. 178-201, first published on December 15, 2010.

26. Emil Pain, "Moscow's North Caucasus Policy Backfires," *Central Asia-Caucasus Analyst*, Vol. 6, No. 13, June 29, 2005, available from *www.cacianalyst.org/?q=node/3151*.

27. Valery Dzutsev, "Another Lost Year for the Kremlin in the North Caucasus: 2010 in Review (Part 1)," *Eurasia Daily Monitor*, Vol. 8, No. 8, January 12, 2011, available from *www. jamestown.org/programs/edm/single/?tx_ttnews%5Btt_news% 5D=37350&tx_ttnews%5BbackPid%5D=27&cHash= 660e50c38e*.

28. Human Rights and Security Initiative, "Violence in the North Caucasus—2009: A Bloody Year," Washington, DC: Center for Strategic and International Studies, January 14, 2010, available from *csis.org/files/publication/100114_Violence_ NorthCaucasus_2009optimize.pdf*.

29. Simon Saradzhyan, "Russia's North Caucasus: the Terrorism Revival," *ISN Insights*, December 23, 2010, available from *www.isn.ethz.ch/isn/Current-Affairs/ISN-Insights/Detail?lng=en &ots627=fce62fe0-528d-4884-9cdf-283c282cf0b2&id=125837&tabid= 125818&contextid734=125837&contextid735=125818*.

30. Human Rights and Security Initiative, "Violence in the North Caucasus—Spring 2010: On the rise, Again?" Washington,

DC: Center for Strategic and International Studies, May 13, 2010, available from *csis.org/files/publication/100513_Violence_in_the_North_Caucasus_Spring_2010.pdf*.

31. Igor Rotar, "Growing Violence in Kabardino-Balkaria Threatens to Destabilize the Northwest Caucasus," *Eurasia Daily Monitor*, Vol. 8, No. 218, December 1, 2011, available from *www.jamestown.org/programs/edm/single/?tx_ttnews%5Btt_news%5D=38732&cHash=530491ac52389684440e5dcc84e128a7*.

32. Emil Souleimanov, "North Ossetia: Jihadization in the Making?" *Central Asia-Caucasus Analyst*, June 8, 2011, available from *www.cacianalyst.org/?q=node/5573*.

33. Graeme P. Herd, "The Russo-Chechen Information Warfare and 9/11: Al-Qaeda through the South Caucasus Looking Glass," *European Security*, Vol. 11, No. 4, 2002.

34. "Basayev's Death May Have Been an Accident," *Prague Watchdog*, July 10, 2006; "Basayev Didn't Save Face," *Kommersant*, July 11, 2006, available from *www.kommersant.com/page.asp?idr=527&id=689111*.

35. Kagarlitsky, *Russia under Yeltsin and Putin*, pp. 229-234.

36. Sanobar Shermatova, "The Secret War between Russian Intelligence Agencies," *Moscow News*, August 8, 2000. Also see Khassan Baiev, Nicholas Daniloff, and Ruth Daniloff, *The Oath: A Surgeon Under Fire*, New York: Walker & Company, 2004.

37. Kevin Daniel Leahy, "Reconciliation between Akhmed Zakayev and Ramzan Kadyrov: A Triumph of Historical Pragmatism?" *Central Asia-Caucasus Analyst*, February 25, 2009, available from *www.cacianalyst.org/?q=node/5048*.

38. Ivan Sukhov, "Chechensky Ochag," *Agenstvo Politicheskikh Novostey*, August 16, 2005, available from *www.apn.ru/publications/article1519.htm*.

39. Ellen Barry and Michael Schwartz, "Killing of Leader's Foes May Test Kremlin's Will," *New York Times*, April 6, 2009, available from *www.nytimes.com/2009/04/07/world/europe/07chechnya.html*.

40. Andrew Osborn, "Ramzan Kadyrov: The Warrior King of Chechnya," *The Independent*, January 4, 2007, available from *www.independent.co.uk/news/people/profiles/ramzan-kadyrov-the-warrior-king-of-chechnya-430738.html*.

41. "Kadyrov Says Putin Saved Chechnya," *RIA Novosti*, April 7, 2009, available from *en.rian.ru/russia/20090407/120959179.html*.

42. "Ramzan Kadyrov: ya sto raz umry za Putina" ("Ramzan Kadyrov: I would die a hundred times for Putin"), *versia.ru*, January 11, 2010, available from *versia.ru/articles/2010/jan/11/kadyrov_interview*.

43. "Kadyrov Vows to Prosecute Federal Commanders for Abuses," *Chechnya Weekly*, December 7, 2006.

44. Kevin Daniel Leahy, "Kadyrov's Bluff," *Central Asia-Caucasus Analyst*, Vol. 8, No. 10, May 17, 2006, p. 7, available from *www.cacianalyst.org/issues/20060517Analyst.pdf*.

45. Kevin Daniel Leahy, "Chechnya's New President: Rational Actor or Ideological Zealot?" *Central Asia-Caucasus Analyst*, Vol. 9, No. 7, April 4, 2007, p. 6, available from *www.cacianalyst.org/files/070404Analyst_0.pdf*.

46. See Human Rights Watch, *"You Dress According to Their Rules": Enforcement of an Islamic Dress Code for Women in Chechnya*, New York: Human Rights Watch, 2011, available from *www.hrw.org/sites/default/files/reports/chechnya0311webwcover.pdf*.

47. See, e.g., Oleg Antonenko, "Chechnya: Gde konchayetsya konstitutsiya i nachinayetsya shariat?" ("Chechnya: where does the constitution end and sharia begin?"), BBC Russian Service, December 26, 2008, available from *news.bbc.co.uk/hi/russian/russia/newsid_7800000/7800125.stm*.

48. Personal communication, Washington, DC, 2006.

49. Jean-Christophe Peuch, "Georgia/Russia: Tbilisi Moves Against Pankisi," *RFE/RL*, August 28, 2002, available from *www.rferl.org/content/article/1100642.html*.

ABOUT THE CONTRIBUTORS

STEPHEN J. BLANK has served as the Strategic Studies Institute's expert on the Soviet bloc and the post-Soviet world since 1989. Prior to that he was Associate Professor of Soviet Studies at the Center for Aerospace Doctrine, Research, and Education, Maxwell Air Force Base, AL; and taught at the University of Texas, San Antonio; and at the University of California, Riverside. Dr. Blank is the editor of *Imperial Decline: Russia's Changing Position in Asia*, coeditor of *Soviet Military and the Future*, and author of *The Sorcerer as Apprentice: Stalin's Commissariat of Nationalities, 1917-1924*. He has also written many articles and conference papers on Russia, the Commonwealth of Independent States, and Eastern European security issues. Dr. Blank's current research deals with proliferation and the revolution in military affairs, and energy and security in Eurasia. His two most recent books are *Russo-Chinese Energy Relations: Politics in Command*, London, UK: Global Markets Briefing, 2006; and *Natural Allies? Regional Security in Asia and Prospects for Indo-American Strategic Cooperation*, Carlisle, PA: Strategic Studies Institute, U.S. Army War College, 2005. Dr. Blank holds a B.A. in history from the University of Pennsylvania, and an M.A. and Ph.D. in history from the University of Chicago.

SVANTE E. CORNELL is Research Director of the Central Asia-Caucasus Institute & Silk Road Studies Program, a Joint Transatlantic Research and Policy Center affiliated with the School of Advanced International Studies (SAIS), Washington, DC, and the Stockholm-based Institute for Security and Development Policy. Dr. Cornell is an Associate Research Professor at SAIS.

GORDON M. HAHN is a Senior Associate (Non-Resident) at the Center for Strategic and International Studies (CSIS) in Washington, DC; a Senior Researcher and Adjunct Professor in the Monterey Terrorism Research and Education Program at the Monterey Institute for International Studies in California; and an Analyst and Consultant for Russia—Other Points of View (*www.russiaotherpointsofview.com*). Dr. Hahn is author of the well-received books, *Russia's Islamic Threat* (Yale University Press, 2007), *Russia's Revolution From Above, 1985-2000* (Transaction Publishers, 2002), and numerous articles in academic journals and other English and Russian language media. He has taught at Boston, American, Stanford, San Jose State, and San Francisco State Universities and as a Fulbright Scholar at Saint Petersburg State University, Russia. Dr. Hahn writes and edits the bimonthly "Islam, Islamism, and Politics in Eurasia Report" published under the auspices of CSIS.

SERGEY MARKEDONOV has been a visiting fellow in the CSIS Russia and Eurasia Program since May 2010. He is an expert on the Caucasus, as well as Black Sea regional security, nationalism, interethnic conflicts, and de-facto states in the post-Soviet area. From 2001 to 2010, he worked as head of the Interethnic Relations Group and deputy director at the Institute for Political and Military Analysis in Moscow. He has held teaching positions at the Russian State University for the Humanities, the Moscow State University, and the Diplomatic Academy. Dr. Markedonov's publications include several books and reports, about 100 academic articles, and more than 500 press pieces. Recently published books and reports include *De facto States of the*

Post-Soviet Space: Particularities of the Nation-Building (Caucasus Institute, 2012), *The Turbulent Eurasia* (Academia, 2010), "The Big Caucasus: Consequences of the 'Five Day War'," and *New Challenges and Prospects* (International Centre for Black Sea Studies, 2009).

www.ingramcontent.com/pod-product-compliance
Lightning Source LLC
Chambersburg PA
CBHW081827280526
45789CB00007B/2373